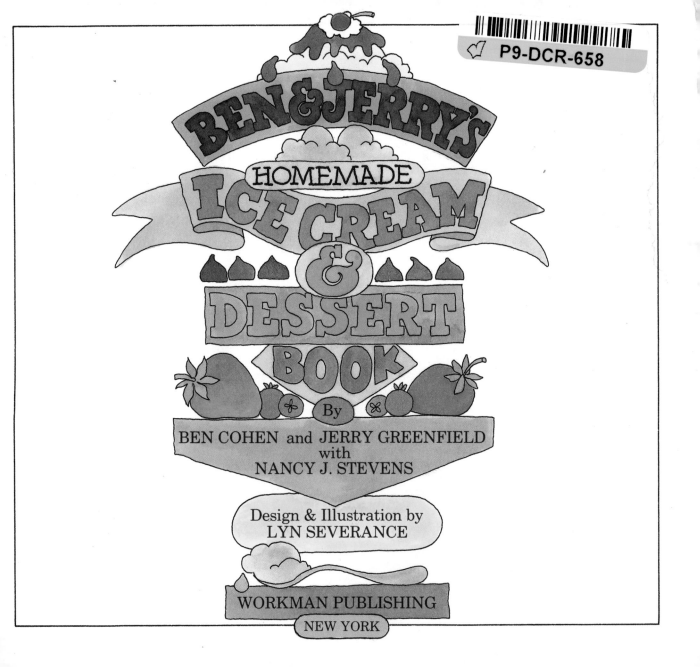

BEN & JERRY'S
HOMEMADE
ICE CREAM
& DESSERT
BOOK

By

BEN COHEN and **JERRY GREENFIELD**
with
NANCY J. STEVENS

Design & Illustration by
LYN SEVERANCE

WORKMAN PUBLISHING

NEW YORK

Special **THANKS** to

Marty Hershkowitz,
Manuel Rockwood,
Bob Cornfield,
Suzanne Rafer,
Peter Workman,
and the entire
ice cream-loving
group at Workman
Publishing.

Library of Congress Cataloging-in-Publication Data
Cohen, Ben (Ben R.)
  Ben & Jerry's homemade ice cream & dessert book.
  1. Ice cream, ices, etc. 2. Desserts. I. Greenfield, Jerry. II. Stevens, Nancy J. III. Title.
IV. Title: Ben and Jerry's homemade ice cream & dessert book.
TX795.C635   1987   641.8'62   86-40543
ISBN-13: 978-0-89480-312-3 (pbk.)

Book design: Lyn Severance

Workman books are available at special discounts when purchased in bulk for premiums and sales promotions as well as for fund-raising or educational use. Special editions or book excerpts can also be created to specification. For details, contact the Special Sales Director at the address below.

Workman Publishing Company, Inc.
225 Varick Street, New York, NY 10014

Manufactured in the United States of America

First printing May 1987
32 31 30 29 28 27

The names of the following ingredients used in certain Ben & Jerry's recipes are registered trademarks of other companies:
5th Avenue® is made by the confectionary division of Luden's, Inc.
Heath® is a registered trademark of L.S. Heath & Sons, Inc.
Kit Kat® is manufactured by H.B. Reese Candy Company, a division of Hershey Foods Corporations.
M&M's® is distributed by M&M Mars, a division of Mars, Inc.
Mystic Mint® is a registered trademark of Nabisco Brands, Inc.
Oreo® is a registered trademark of Nabisco Brands, Inc.
Post® Grape-Nuts® is manufactured by General Foods Corporation.
Reese's® Peanut Butter Cups® are manufactured by H.B. Reese Candy Company, a division of Hershey Foods Corporation.
Rolo® Cups are manufactured by Hershey Chocolate Company, a division of Hershey Foods Corporation.

CONTENTS

Our Story *by Ben* 5
Ice Cream Theory *by Jerry* 17
Recipes—
   Sweet Cream Bases 28
   11 Greatest Hits 31
   Chocolate Ice Creams 43
   Fruit Flavors 49
   Downtown Specials 61
   Cookies and Candies 79
   Sorbets 89
   The Bakery 97
   Sundaes & Concoctions 107
   Sauces 119
   Drinks 123
Index 126

Our Story

Y ou couldn't really say we started out small...

…since we'd been shopping in the chubby department from the age of six. When Jerry and I first met in seventh grade gym class, we were already the two widest kids on the field and the only ones who couldn't run a mile in seven minutes.

We became best friends. We shared many interests, but most of all, a deep and sincere appreciation of good food and lots of it. One summer, I got a job driving an ice cream truck on Long Island for which I earned $100 a week and as much free ice cream as I could eat. I thought this was a great deal and convinced Jerry to sign up for a neighboring route, but he quit after one day. He didn't think he had much of a future in ice cream. He set his sights instead on the medical profession.

After high school, we went our separate ways. Jerry headed west to Oberlin College to study pre-med, and I went north to Colgate. I didn't really want to go to college, and, after a year and a half, I dropped out and traveled around the country. I visited Jerry in Ohio and got a night job selling sandwiches in the dorms. Jerry had just finished a half-credit course in Carnival Techniques and had distinguished himself in fire-eating and cinder-block smashing. Because he was so eager to demonstrate his prowess, I volunteered to be the smashee. I wrapped myself up in a sheet, swami-style, mumbled some metabolic mantras, and ventured out on campus where Jerry and his sledgehammer calmly waited. I lay down; he placed the cinder block on my bare belly and then, in one smash, pulverized it to smithereens. Thus was born Habeeni Ben Coheeni, Indian mystic madman, willing and able to withstand the merciless sledgehammer.

After a while, I decided to go back to college and enrolled in Skidmore College, where I studied such unorthodox subjects as pottery and organic gardening. Eventually, I dropped out for good and took up a series of odd jobs ranging from night mopper at Friendly's, taxi driver in Manhattan, kitchen assistant at Mrs. London's Bake Shop (I separated the eggs), and Pinkerton night guard at the Saratoga Race Track (I stood by a shack in the middle of the track guarding an empty canoe with a covered holster, but no gun). None of these jobs ever lasted more than a few months. Finally, I ended up in a small town in upstate New York called Paradox, working with emotionally disturbed children.

Meanwhile, Jerry had graduated but didn't get into medical school. He took a job as a lab technician in North Carolina and reapplied, only to be turned down again. By this time, we had both realized we really weren't getting where we wanted to go. So we decided to change our courses and head there together. We weren't interested in making a lot of money; we just wanted to do something that would be fun. Our business goals were modest, but specific: We wanted to be our own bosses and work exactly when, where, and how we wanted.

Starting Up

At that time, my two favorite foods were bagels and ice cream, so I thought it would be great to open a little restaurant that would sell either one. We considered starting a delivery service called U.B.S., short for United Bagel Service, and looked into buying a bagel machine. After one telephone call to price the equipment, we decided we were in the ice cream business.

We soon understood that in order to do this right, we needed to know how to make ice cream. We also needed to find a nice small town that lacked a homemade ice cream parlor. So the research began.

We wanted to settle in a rural college town, preferably one that was warm, so everyone would want to eat a lot of ice cream all year round. We decided to choose our location based on three key factors: a healthy student population, a good-size town population, and a moderate climate.

Coheeni's First Law

We considered a few towns in Massachusetts but decided they were too seasonal for our needs. At a friend's suggestion, we took a look at Burlington, Vermont. It had the right number of students, and its population was growing at a good rate. It didn't already have an ice cream parlor. What it did have was an average of 161 days a year when the temperature plunged below freezing and a total winter snow accumulation of five feet (not counting a spring accumulation of 13 inches). That bothered us until I came up with the

Internal-External Temperature Differential and Equalization Theory (later to become Coheeni's First Law of Ice-Cream-Eating Dynamics). Herein I explained that the apparent cold that the body feels in cold climates is based on the difference between the internal body temperature and the external temperature. By lowering the internal temperature (through eating cold things in the winter), the internal temperature drops and the body feels comparative warmth. We discovered that a healthy, daily intake of cold ice cream not only helped to reduce that difference, but it also helped to make the frigid winter months much more bearable, if not downright pleasant.

So Burlington it was. We moved there in the early fall, which is never a bad time in New England, with its incredible colors, partially sunny skies, and crisp, clean (did I say cold?) air. We found an old abandoned gasoline station that was literally falling apart. You could see daylight through the roof; there were six inches of ice on the floor, hardly any walls, no ceiling, and whatever was left standing was badly water damaged. But it was a great location. We saw its potential and signed a lease for the first home of Ben & Jerry's. We agreed that it sounded better than Jerry & Ben's. Since my name came first, Jerry became president and I became vice president.

Learning the Food Business

It was several months before we could take occupancy and begin our renovation. So in the interim, we decided to learn more about the food business by setting up a hot drink stand for the Christmas shopping season in the basement of Bennington Potters North, a ceramic and gift shop in downtown Burlington. There, side by side with chipped and slightly irregular pottery seconds, we served hot cider, freshly brewed coffee, herbal tea, and homemade eggnog and entertained our customers with a variety of jigsaw puzzles and games like "Shoot the Moon." Every night, I prepared batches of oatmeal cookie batter, and, during the day, we baked them in the toaster oven installed on one of the basement tables.

People started coming from nearby shops just to get the hot fresh cookies. But by that time, we were giving most of them away to anyone who could put together three jigsaw puzzle pieces or tell us a funny joke. Much later, more sophisticated people told us that giving away cookies was a great "consumer incentive," but for us, it was just a way to make new friends. It was also the birth of one of our longest lasting and most popular traditions—giving things away.

Getting Serious

After Christmas, when it really got cold, Jerry and I holed up in the house we were renting on an island in Lake Champlain. We bought an old player piano in pieces and began to reassemble it. We also bought a big, blue college-level textbook called *Ice Cream* by Wendell S. Arbuckle, the father of modern American ice cream, and a used old-fashioned White Mountain ice cream maker (which was described as obsolete and unreliable in our textbook). We began experimenting. Sometimes the ice cream was rich and creamy, sometimes it bounced and stretched. In the end, it really didn't matter, because except for one particularly weird batch of rum raisin, we always ate it all.

Then we really decided to get serious. We each chipped in $2.50 for an ice-cream-making correspondence course from Pennsylvania State University. We bought fresh cream, milk, and eggs, and bags of rock salt for the ice cream maker. We chopped the ice right out of the lake. Every day, we studied our lessons and tried to apply them to our own ice cream making. I didn't understand the technical part too well, but with Jerry's background in chemistry, it was a cinch for him. Things were looking good. We got 100 percent on all our tests (cheating wasn't possible since they were all open-book exams), and, at the end of fourteen weeks, we were officially qualified to make ice cream.

In early March, we pooled our slim resources—$4,000 from Jerry's savings, $2,000 from my savings, an additional $2,000 from my father, and $4,000 from our local banker—and began renovating the gas station. With more than a little help from our friends Daryl, Mumpo, and Vinnie, we patched the

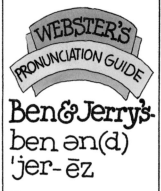

WEBSTER'S PRONUNCIATION GUIDE

Ben&Jerry's-
ben ən(d) 'jer- ēz

Ben says:

People always ask me why our ice cream is so different from all those other brands out there. Easy, it's the only superpremium ice cream you can pronounce.

roof, put up new walls and a ceiling, installed new electrical wiring and did some of the plumbing work. Then we had a painting party and transformed the place into a vision in orange and white. Then we had another painting party because we didn't like the orange. (I guess we didn't do everything right the first time.)

Jerry and I began reading the newspaper for announcements of restaurant auctions where we hoped to pick up some good, used equipment at fairly reasonable prices. Our first time out, we drove four hours to a small, remote town in New Hampshire and bought everything we needed dirt cheap. We also bought a bunch of unmatched chairs, a few big tables (that we later sawed up into many little tables), and various irresistible odd lots, like one memorable antique hospital bed that's still in my house.

We opened our doors on May 5, 1978. Ben & Jerry's was a decidedly funky and original place. We brought in the player piano, and Don Rose, a friend of ours, would come by and play his honky-tonk music to please the crowd and pace our scoopers. His *Ice Cream Blues* ("I like homemade ice cream but I don't like standing in line. Down at Ben & Jerry's, well, I'll wait any old time. Diddy wah, diddy wah doooo. . .") was a great hit. One day, Jerry went over to Don, put his arm around his shoulder, and announced that he had just become the first member of the Free Ice Cream For Life Club.

People didn't mind standing on line for ice cream, especially when Don Rose was at the keyboard. For a long time, we couldn't believe how well everything was going. At first, Jerry was worried that our customers were just humoring us because they didn't want to hurt our feelings. The service ranged from poor to inconsistent, at its very best. Jerry wondered whether our popularity was due to the kindness of the Burlington populace.

The Art of Scooping
Aim for smooth, long lines when scooping and never use a wet scoop—the water freezes to a thin layer of ice and will ruin the texture of the ice cream you are serving.

More Chunks, Less Bunk

Jerry got to the point where the ice cream he was making was pretty good, but there just weren't enough big chunks in it for my taste.

"You've got all these little flecks in there, Jerry," I'd say to him. "It's my feeling that if you get a chunk in your ice cream, it has to be a really big one."

I always liked the contrast between smooth ice cream and a fairly frequent humongous chunk. But Jerry had a real feeling about consistency. He didn't want any particular spoonful to be without several chunks, even if that meant they had to be small. He didn't want to run the risk of a customer taking a spoonful of our ice cream and that spoonful not having any chunks at all. I was willing to take that risk because I knew that the very next spoonful would contain a really good, big one, the kind of huge chunk you could bust your spoon on.

After considerable discussion, we decided there was only one way to go. We'd make all our ice cream with big chunks and lots and lots of them. It was a compromise, but a pretty good one.

We started out making four-gallon batches that would serve up to 100 people, but, shortly after we opened, we were scooping 1,000 cones a day, and Jerry was working nonstop behind the dasher. One hot summer day, we ran out of ice cream long before closing time, and the International No Ice Cream sign (an ice cream cone with a slash through it) appeared over the door. Running out of ice cream meant that batches of even our weirdest and possibly least delicious flavor experiments (i.e., our mistakes), such as Lemon Peppermint Carob Chip, disappeared as soon as they were put out. Jerry was finally reassured. People liked our ice cream.

On the House

Jerry and I have always liked to give things away; so on our first anniversary, we threw open the doors of the gas station and gave everyone free ice cream cones. On Mother's Day, we gave free cones to all mothers and two cones to obviously pregnant women. We also joined in community celebrations in and around Burlington. For one downtown festival, we staged our

On Abundance

Our guiding principle is one of abundance. Whenever possible, we serve a generous scoop of ice cream, a glorious plop of hot fudge sauce, a humongous chunk of chocolate. We like our customers to feel that they're treating themselves well.

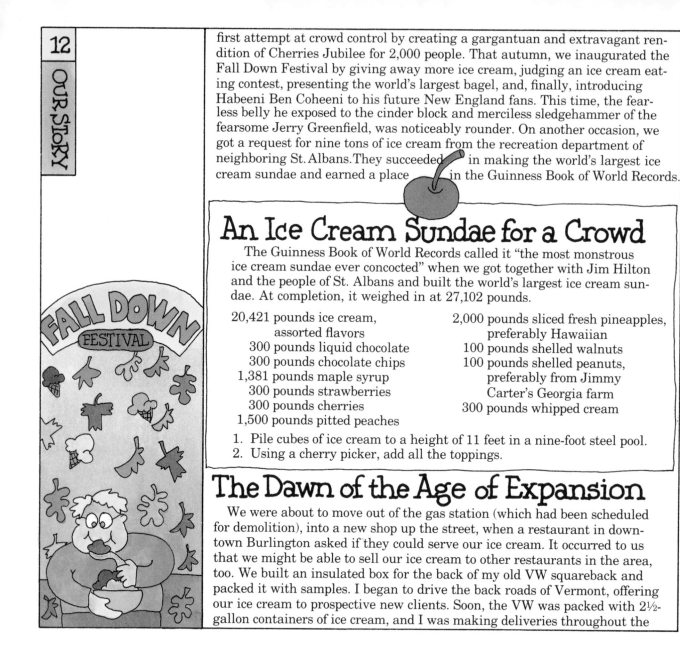

first attempt at crowd control by creating a gargantuan and extravagant rendition of Cherries Jubilee for 2,000 people. That autumn, we inaugurated the Fall Down Festival by giving away more ice cream, judging an ice cream eating contest, presenting the world's largest bagel, and, finally, introducing Habeeni Ben Coheeni to his future New England fans. This time, the fearless belly he exposed to the cinder block and merciless sledgehammer of the fearsome Jerry Greenfield, was noticeably rounder. On another occasion, we got a request for nine tons of ice cream from the recreation department of neighboring St. Albans. They succeeded in making the world's largest ice cream sundae and earned a place in the Guinness Book of World Records.

An Ice Cream Sundae for a Crowd

The Guinness Book of World Records called it "the most monstrous ice cream sundae ever concocted" when we got together with Jim Hilton and the people of St. Albans and built the world's largest ice cream sundae. At completion, it weighed in at 27,102 pounds.

20,421 pounds ice cream, assorted flavors
300 pounds liquid chocolate
300 pounds chocolate chips
1,381 pounds maple syrup
300 pounds strawberries
300 pounds cherries
1,500 pounds pitted peaches

2,000 pounds sliced fresh pineapples, preferably Hawaiian
100 pounds shelled walnuts
100 pounds shelled peanuts, preferably from Jimmy Carter's Georgia farm
300 pounds whipped cream

1. Pile cubes of ice cream to a height of 11 feet in a nine-foot steel pool.
2. Using a cherry picker, add all the toppings.

The Dawn of the Age of Expansion

We were about to move out of the gas station (which had been scheduled for demolition), into a new shop up the street, when a restaurant in downtown Burlington asked if they could serve our ice cream. It occurred to us that we might be able to sell our ice cream to other restaurants in the area, too. We built an insulated box for the back of my old VW squareback and packed it with samples. I began to drive the back roads of Vermont, offering our ice cream to prospective new clients. Soon, the VW was packed with 2½-gallon containers of ice cream, and I was making deliveries throughout the state, driving as fast as my car would go (and of course, as fast as Vermont law permits), to keep the ice cream from melting. After a year, business was booming. We rented additional manufacturing space, bought a used 1969 ice cream truck, and painted on it two huge arms that wrapped around the sides and met in the back, grasping giant ice cream cones. Things were great. Twelve people were working for us downtown, Jerry was coming up with ever stranger flavors, and I had become a traveling salesman.

A Pint-Size Move

It was fun, but it didn't take much mathematical wizardry to realize that we weren't making any money. All our profits went into the truck, which was in a constant state of disrepair. Since we couldn't afford a new one, we simply had to increase our road sales. The idea of selling our ice cream in pint containers to all the Mom-and-Pop grocery stores I passed on my delivery routes seemed like a long shot, but it was worth a try. It was, however, a much bigger undertaking than we had first imagined. We would have to find a larger space to produce the ice cream. And then we would need $15,000 (which was $20,000 more than we had made the previous year) just for the printed cardboard containers alone. We had to try it, so we borrowed the money, moved into our first plant, and placed our first container order.

On my first day out, I signed ten groceries. After four weeks, my list of fifty accounts jumped to two hundred. In six months, we were selling ice cream to nine Grand Union supermarkets. Four months later, another nine Grand Unions signed up. By the end of the year, our ice cream was in all the Grand Unions in Vermont.

"I tell you, the butter pecan is serious ice cream."—Bryant Gumbel, Today show.

Suddenly, every time we looked around, Ben & Jerry's was gaining on us. The 750-square-foot production area of our new plant had once been a spool and bobbin mill. We installed a walk-in cooler and walk-in freezer and produced 100 gallons of ice cream a day. It began to look like we were in the ice cream manufacturing business. We still were our own bosses and we still worked whenever we wanted, which was simply all the time, every minute of every waking hour. It was exhilarating.

One day, Jerry announced that he had finished some serious soul searching. His girlfriend Elizabeth wanted to continue her graduate studies in Arizona, so he thought it would be a good opportunity for him to step away from ice cream production for a while (and maybe lose some of the sixty pounds he had acquired in the name of quality control). He opted for "early retirement," promising to come back to Vermont every summer to participate in community celebrations, including the ever-popular Dramatic Sledgehammer Smashing.

Just before Jerry left, the business started growing again, and Chico Lager, a reasonably thin guy with a bushy mustache, joined us as general manager. Not only was Chico our friend—we used to hang out in his bar back when we had time to hang out in bars—but he also had a degree in business administration. He spent the first two months just going through drawers and drawers of papers and unopened envelopes, including one with a two-year-old tax refund check. Almost everything in our office was neatly stacked in file folders labeled "To Be Filed." Chico tried to set up systems for us, and, much to our surprise, we learned that we were operating a million-dollar-a-year business. We were distributing our ice cream in upstate New York, New Hampshire, and Maine. We had just moved into a 3,000-foot plant behind a local car dealership in South Burlington, and our sales continued to double every year.

We Defy the Odds / A Cautionary Tale

So many people in Vermont loved our Heath Bar Crunch that we thought it was time to introduce our euphoric flavors to the rest of the world. We decided to test the waters in Boston, and if that worked, we could go for the big time—national distribution. But as Chico coolly put it, as soon as Ben & Jerry's made its Boston debut, we were almost slaughtered. It wasn't that people there didn't like our ice cream. They loved it. One day our distributors informed us that they could no longer distribute our ice cream there. Why not? we asked. They explained that Pillsbury, the food conglomerate that had just bought Häagen-Dazs ice cream, had told them to drop Ben & Jerry's or lose Häagen-Dazs. You represent a very small part of our business, the distributor said, and Häagen-Dazs represents a very large part.

We sat there and laughed. Then we went back home and realized just what it all meant. And we thought maybe we should cry. "They're going for our throats," said Chico. Pure and simple. Not only was this new development life threatening, but it was probably illegal.

Doughboy Busters

We hired the best anti-trust lawyer we could afford, but we knew that a little company with twenty-three employees could not hold its own against a company with annual sales of four billion dollars. Then we decided to try a few tactics of our own and take the issue directly to the people. "What's the Doughboy Afraid Of?" became our rallying cry. We printed it on bumper stickers, our pints, and bus posters and even flew it on banners over Patriots games in Boston. We placed an ad in *Rolling Stone* that asked readers to

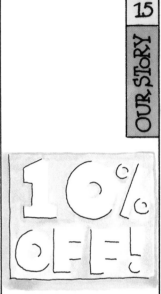

January White Sale
Every January, the temperature in Burlington hovers around 16 degrees above zero and the days get very, very short. That's when we run our famous storewide White Sale. Everything white gets marked down ten percent.

What's the Doughboy Afraid of?

"help two Vermont hippies battle the giant Pillsbury Corporation" by sending $1.00 for a "What's the Doughboy Afraid Of" bumper sticker. In addition, we stickered our pints with a toll-free Doughboy Hotline number. Our free Doughboy kit came with instructions for participating in our letter-writing campaign to the president of Pillsbury. We received most of our calls between midnight and 2 a.m., from what sounded like very happy consumers. In our downtown store, we sold T-shirts with "Ben & Jerry's Legal Defense Fund— Major Contributor" emblazoned across the back. From all parts of Vermont, school children volunteered to form gangs of Doughboy Busters.

But our saving grace was Jerry, who appeared unexpectedly, a tanned and slender vision from Arizona, ready to call a temporary halt to his self-imposed retirement. He flew to Minneapolis and, holding a "What's the Doughboy Afraid Of?" placard, unstintingly walked a one-man picket in front of Pillsbury's worldwide headquarters. He distributed free literature and chatted amiably with the bewildered employees. After a week's service, Jerry disappeared again out west.

Of course there's a happy ending. We settled our lawsuit out of court. We built a new, even bigger plant in nearby Waterbury, we still make Vermont's finest all-natural ice cream, and we still give lots of it away. At last count, we were selling ice cream up and down the East Coast, West Coast, and throughout much of the Midwest.

And best of all, after two years in the sunny Southwest, Jerry decided he really did miss those New England winters. He showed up at the new plant one day wearing a conspiratorial grin and a T-shirt with a picture of a green turtle labeled Vermont. Below that, it read "What is green and moves backwards?" We gave him a new Ben & Jerry's T-shirt and welcomed him home.

ICE CREAM THEORY

When Ben & I first set out to make ice cream...

...we were unencumbered by experience and weren't about to let the myth of expertise get in our way. We visited a lot of ice cream parlors to get an idea of how other people's ice cream tasted, bought a few books, and took a correspondence course in ice cream making. Then we started experimenting. We learned two lessons right away. First, you don't have to be a pro to make incredibly delicious ice cream. You just need the best ingredients, great recipes, a devotion to quality, a dependable ice cream maker, and a sense of adventure. (Forget caution!) Second, there's no such thing as an unredeemingly bad batch of homemade ice cream. This is an undertaking where success is rampant and failures are few and far between. After ten years behind the dasher, it's my firm belief that if you start with the right stuff, get it cold enough, and take care in what you do, you'll come out with something good.

The truth about ice cream is that it is easy to make and there are no secrets. The main advantage to making your own ice cream is that you can put whatever you want into it and make it just the way you like it.

The Sweet Cream Base

Ice cream is basically a sweetened, flavored, frozen dairy product made with cream and milk. The butterfat content of the dairy products makes the ice cream rich and creamy. Butterfat is found in differing amounts in heavy cream, light cream, half-and-half, and milk. Ice cream also contains a proportion of nonfat solids (which are found in whole, skimmed, and condensed milk) to give it body. Eggs may be added for even more richness. Sugar or honey sweetens it.

You can make ice cream with only these ingredients and it will taste fine. In the ice cream business, this is referred to as the basic mix or the sweet cream mix, meaning that it has no added flavoring. It is simply the taste of fresh sweet cream after freezing. We make a flavor called Sweet Cream Oreo, which is a sweet cream mix with chopped-up Oreos thrown in at the last minute. Most of the time, however, the sweet cream mix is used as a base to which we add different flavorings and taste sensations.

The Butterfat Chart indicates the proportions of butterfat found in commonly available sources of cream or milk. Our three sweet cream bases (see pages 28–29) contain different proportions of butterfat. Experiment with all three, and then, if you prefer, use the chart to customize your own ice cream base.

For the ultimate in rich, creamy ice cream, use Sweet Cream Base 1, which has the highest amount of heavy cream. If you prefer something lighter and less caloric, increase the proportion of milk to heavy cream. Basically, you can combine different amounts of cream and milk to suit your taste, mood, or diet. You can make ice cream with canned evaporated milk or canned sweetened condensed milk (and we do give you such a recipe), but this is the recipe of last resort. Save it for those times when it's 20 degrees below, the wind is howling, there's three feet of snow out the front door, and there's no fresh milk in the refrigerator. Believe me, we've had days like that!

Butterfat Chart

	Percentage of Butterfat
Heavy Cream	36%
Whipping cream Light whipping cream Medium cream	30 to 36%
Light cream	18 to 30%
Half-and-half Coffee creamer Coffee cereal special	10½ to 18%
Sweetened condensed whole milk	9% and 40% additional sugar
Evaporated milk	8% and 50% less water
Milk	3 to 4%
Low-fat milk	0.5 to 2%
Skim milk	less than 0.5%

Information for this chart was obtained from Regulations Bulletin #54, published in 1984 by the Commissioner of Agriculture, Vermont.

Sweeteners

Ice cream requires some sort of sweetener whether it be sugar, honey, or maple syrup. We always use pure cane sugar, because our experience tells us that it's not possible to make a better ice cream with any other sweetener.

If you prefer the taste of honey, you can substitute it for sugar on a one-to-one basis. Some people feel that honey is sweeter than sugar, others claim the opposite. The literature on the subject is conflicting. The darker the honey, the stronger the flavoring, so keep in mind that honey-sweetened ice cream will always have a slightly detectable honey taste.

When we first opened our store in the gas station, we used honey in several "health food" flavors, but after the ice cream hardened, we found that the texture was crumbly and the honey flavor overpowering. Since then, we've abandoned honey in favor of pure cane sugar.

Maple syrup lends a slight maple flavor to the ice cream. If this is what you want, use Grade A light amber maple syrup and substitute it at a ratio of 1 cup maple syrup for each ¾ cup sugar. Because of maple syrup's high water content, it will dilute the concentration of butterfat in the ice cream mix and affect the final richness and texture of the finished product. Therefore, always be sure to use it in a mix with the highest butterfat content. You may even consider increasing the proportion of butterfat in the mix by reducing the amount of milk and adding more cream. When we make Honey Apple Raisin Walnut Ice Cream or Maple Walnut Ice Cream, we always start with our richest cream base.

Corn syrup adds both sweetness and body to frozen desserts. It works well with fruit sorbets, but we don't use it in our ice cream. Many commercial ice creams use corn syrup because it's a cheap source of sweetness and body. We never recommend it for making ice cream.

As for artificial sweeteners, we would never use them and don't recommend them for making homemade ice cream or sorbets.

Eggs

Most homemade ice cream has eggs or egg yolks that act as an emulsifying agent suspending the butterfat particles. (Many commercial ice creams use polysorbate 80.) Eggs also add texture to ice cream and improve its whipping ability. All in all, they help make a richer, creamier ice cream that holds up better in storage. If you have personal or dietary objections to using eggs, you can make your ice cream without them (see Sweet Cream Bases 2 and 3). Just be sure to eat it all right away, because it won't store well.

The Hidden Ingredient

When you freeze the sweet cream base in your ice cream maker, you are adding an invisible but essential ingredient—air. All ice cream has some amount of air. If ice cream had no air at all, it would be a solid frozen block and totally unpalatable.

The higher the quality of the ice cream, the smaller the amount of air. Our superpremium ice cream is only 20 percent air and weighs about 7½ pounds per gallon. Most commercial ice creams contain 50 percent air, which is the legal limit, and weigh 4½ pounds per gallon. Every spoonful of that kind of ice cream is half air, half ice cream.

In the lingo of the ice cream business, this air is called overrun. It is stirred into the ice cream during the freezing process. You can control the overrun in your ice cream to some extent by overfilling the canister with the sweet cream mix at the start. Most ice-cream-maker manufacturers recommend filling the canister anywhere from one-half to two-thirds full. If you want less air, you can fill it three-quarters full. That means you're not going to have more than 25 percent air whipped into your ice cream.

Ice Crystals

All ice cream is frozen according to the same principles, whether it is made at home with a quart-size ice cream maker or in a manufacturing plant with the most technologically advanced commercial equipment. There is always a freezing agent, and this freezing agent must never come in direct contact with the ice cream mix. Some machines use rock salt or table salt and ice as the freezing agent. Others use either a eutectic solution or Freon gas inside the canister to lower the freezing point.

Problems with Your Ice Cream?

If your ice cream isn't freezing to your satisfaction, maybe:

- *the ingredients weren't cold enough;*

- *the dasher blades in your ice cream maker aren't sharp enough or they are not making close enough contact with the sides of the canister;*

- *the dasher is being turned too quickly or in the wrong direction;*

- *you're not using enough salt.*

No matter how you freeze your ice cream, there will always be ice crystals in it. The idea is to make them so small that they will not be detectable on the tongue. The faster you freeze your mix, the smaller the ice crystals will be and the smoother and creamier the ice cream will taste. Some commercial machines in ice cream plants can turn out a batch of ice cream from the liquid mix to the finished semifrozen state in 30 seconds. The ice crystals are barely perceptible.

When making ice cream at home, freezing usually takes from twenty to thirty minutes, but, if you follow the manufacturer's directions, your ice cream can be incredibly smooth and creamy.

SOFT OR HARD ICE CREAM?

Fresh ice cream, whether made at home or in a factory, is initially a soft product. You can get it harder by letting your ice cream sit longer in the ice cream maker before serving or by packing it in an airtight container and placing it in the freezer. Just be aware that ice cream hardened in a home freezer tends to get icy.

Flavorings

Some flavorings, such as vanilla or melted chocolate, are added at the beginning of the freezing process. Other denser ingredients, such as Heath Bars or fresh raspberries, are added just moments before the ice cream is ready. Vanilla is the most popular flavor in the world, and it is found in almost 75 percent of all ice cream. Chocolate is the second most popular. Strawberry comes in third. After that, different regions of the country start battling it out with their favorites. Politicians in Vermont like Maple Walnut Ice Cream.

Adding a flavoring with a high moisture or water content will dilute the sweet cream mix and affect the body and texture of the finished ice cream. When making fruit-flavored ice creams, for example, we always recommend starting with Sweet Cream Base 1 or a similar high-butterfat mix.

Salt

Salt is sometimes added to vanilla and chocolate ice cream in very small amounts as a flavor enhancer. It is not necessary and doesn't improve the texture of the ice cream. I personally don't use it, because I'd rather keep salt out of my ice cream if I can. Once again, it's a matter of personal taste.

In this book, there are only two recipes that call for salt. One is Butter Pecan Ice Cream; here, the extra salt is essential to the flavor of the roasted pecans. The other recipe is Ben's Chocolate Ice Cream. This may be the richest, most chocolaty chocolate ice cream you'll ever taste. Ben claims that he doesn't have a very acute sense of taste, so it takes a strong dose of any flavor to get a response from him. In this case, he believes that the salt helps deliver the heavy-flavored chocolate in its full glory.

Liqueur

Alcohol depresses the freezing point of ice cream. Therefore, when you add a liqueur to your basic mix, it will always take longer to freeze and the finished ice cream will always be softer than other ice creams.

Adding the right amount of liqueur is a tricky, self-limiting proposition. If you put too much into the mix, the ice cream won't freeze. Put in enough so that you can just begin to taste the liqueur. Trust the recipe. Whenever you flavor an ice cream with liqueur, you'll either end up with a subtly flavored ice cream or an unfreezable sweet cream liquid mix that reeks of alcohol. This is one place where I take my measurements very seriously!

Fruit

Most fruit has a high proportion of water in it, so we advise using a sweet cream mix with the highest proportion of butterfat, such as Sweet Cream Base 1. For certain fruits, it helps quite a bit if you can prepare them in advance, sometimes just a few hours beforehand, sometimes as much as a day before.

Usually, we cut up fresh fruit, add sugar, and chill the mixture in the refrigerator in a covered bowl. Every half hour or so, we toss the fruit. When the fruit and sugar mingle, they combine and bring out the best in each other. The sugar lowers the freezing point of the fruit and prevents it from becoming too icy when added to the ice cream. The sugar also extracts the fruit's natural juices and helps flavor the ice cream during the freezing process.

Heath Bars Are More Hygroscopic Than Grape-Nuts . . .

Hygroscopic ingredients, such as chopped Heath Bars, readily take up moisture and tend to retain it. Whenever you put them in ice cream, they will change its texture, usually for the better. By the same token, any hydroscopic ingredient will get soft and moist and lose some of its crunch.

A Pint-Size Batch

All the recipes in this book yield 1 quart of ice cream, but they can be easily adapted to the pint-size ice cream makers. Just halve all the ingredients, then freeze according to the manufacturer's instructions.

1/2

Cookies & Candies

When adding chunks like Heath Bars or Oreo cookies to your ice cream, always add them to the canister just before the ice cream is completely frozen. If you put them in at the beginning of the freezing process, they will simply sink to the bottom and never get mixed in with the ice cream.

Choosing the right ingredients to add to your ice cream is another area that invites experimentation. Here's a good exercise in R&D (Research and Development): Put on sensible shoes, do some warm-up stretches (this will stimulate your appetite), and slowly push a shopping cart down the aisles of your local supermarket. You'll soon be ready to graduate to specialty food stores and gourmet shops.

Sweet Cream Bases

This, our most popular base, has creamy texture, medium body, and a subtle, understated taste. It's especially good as a background for fruit, cookies, and candy.

2 large eggs
¾ cup sugar

2 cups heavy or whipping cream
1 cup milk

Whisk the eggs in a mixing bowl until light and fluffy, 1 to 2 minutes. Whisk in the sugar, a little at a time, then continue whisking until completely blended, about 1 minute more. Pour in the cream and milk and whisk to blend.

Makes 1 quart

This simple recipe is made with a minimum of ingredients and requires no cooking. It makes a very creamy ice cream with 25 percent butterfat, but it does not store well in home freezers, so be prepared to eat it all.

2 cups heavy or whipping cream *⅔ cup half-and-half*
¾ cup sugar

Pour the cream into a mixing bowl. Whisk in the sugar, a little at a time, then continue whisking until completely blended, about 1 minute more. Pour in the half-and-half and whisk to blend.

Makes 1 quart

This recipe makes a less creamy, less rich ice cream. Ben likes the slightly "cooked" flavor of the sweetened condensed milk.

2 cups light cream *1 cup sweetened condensed milk, cold*

Whisk the light cream and the sweetened condensed milk together in a mixing bowl until blended.

Makes 1 quart

GREATEST Hits

11

ur downtown store was always our working lab. It's here that we perfected Heath Bar Crunch and Oreo Mint Ice Cream and reluctantly relinquished Lemon Peppermint Carob Chip. Because our customers were always willing to subject themselves to new taste sensations, no batch ever lasted very long. And with this freedom, we flourished.

Heath Bar Crunch

Jerry says:

Since Ben had been experimenting with candy and ice cream combinations from the age of five, I was not surprised when he suggested we try an ice cream made with Heath Bars. The concept was good—it was the execution that challenged us.

We started by buying individual bars, and it became my job to cut them, two at a time, into thirds. I chopped away on a plastic cutting board, using a grid as my guideline. As the demand for the flavor grew, we began buying the bars in

(Continued on next page)

Our all-time best-selling flavor. When we give away free cones, we often set up a "Heath Bar Crunch Express Line."

4 original Heath Bars
    (1⅛ ounces each)
2 large eggs

¾ cup sugar
2 cups heavy or whipping cream
1 cup milk
2 teaspoons vanilla extract

1. Using a sharp knife, cut the candy bars into ½- to 1-inch chunks. You should have about 1 cup. Place the chunks in a bowl, cover, and freeze.

2. Whisk the eggs in a mixing bowl until light and fluffy, 1 to 2 minutes. Whisk in the sugar, a little at a time, then continue whisking until completely blended, about 1 minute more. Pour in the cream, milk, vanilla extract, and whisk to blend.

3. Transfer the mixture to an ice cream maker and freeze following the manufacturer's instructions.

4. After the ice cream stiffens (about 2 minutes before it is done), add the candy, then continue freezing until the ice cream is ready.

Makes generous 1 quart

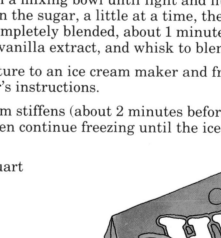

Heath® is a registered trademark of L.S. Heath & Sons, Inc.

We've converted quite a few dyed-in-the-wool Heath Bar Crunch fans since introducing Coffee Heath Bar Crunch.

4 original Heath Bars
  (1⅛ ounces each)
2 large eggs
¾ cup sugar

2 cups heavy or whipping cream
1 cup milk
3 tablespoons good-quality
  freeze-dried coffee

1. Using a sharp knife, cut the candy bars into ½- to 1-inch chunks. You should have about 1 cup. Place the chunks in a bowl, cover and freeze.

2. Whisk the eggs in a mixing bowl until light and fluffy, 1 to 2 minutes. Whisk in the sugar, a little at a time, then continue whisking until completely blended, about 1 minute more. Add the cream, milk, and 2 tablespoons of the coffee and whisk just until blended.

3. Transfer the mixture to an ice cream maker and freeze following the manufacturer's instructions.

4. After the ice cream stiffens (about 2 minutes before it is done), add the candy and remaining 1 tablespoon coffee, then continue freezing until the ice cream is ready.

Makes generous 1 quart

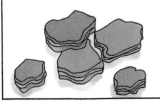

twenty-pound boxes. At first, I continued to cut each one by hand, the old-fashioned way. Then one day, out of frustration at spending the better part of my life hand-chopping Heath Bars, I threw a box down onto the floor, shattering the bars inside. That worked pretty well, both for the candy and for my frustration. Next we tried smashing the box with a plastic mallet. Finally, through trial and error, we discovered that a frozen twenty-pound box of Heath Bars dropped from a six-foot stepladder cracked to the perfect size.

New York Super Fudge Chunk

New York Super Fudge Chunk was developed as a regional flavor for the sophisticated New York palate. After coming up with several variations in our Burlington lab, we packed the samples in dry ice and shipped them by bus to our New York consultants, a group of musicians on Manhattan's Upper West Side. Following several weeks of refinement and discussion, we agreed upon this final recipe—a chocolate lover's dream.

*¼ cup coarsely chopped
   white chocolate*
*¼ cup coarsely chopped
   semisweet chocolate*
¼ cup chopped pecan halves
¼ cup coarsely chopped walnuts
*¼ cup halved chocolate-covered
   almonds*

4 ounces unsweetened chocolate
1 cup milk
2 large eggs
1 cup sugar
1 cup heavy or whipping cream
1 teaspoon vanilla extract
1 pinch salt

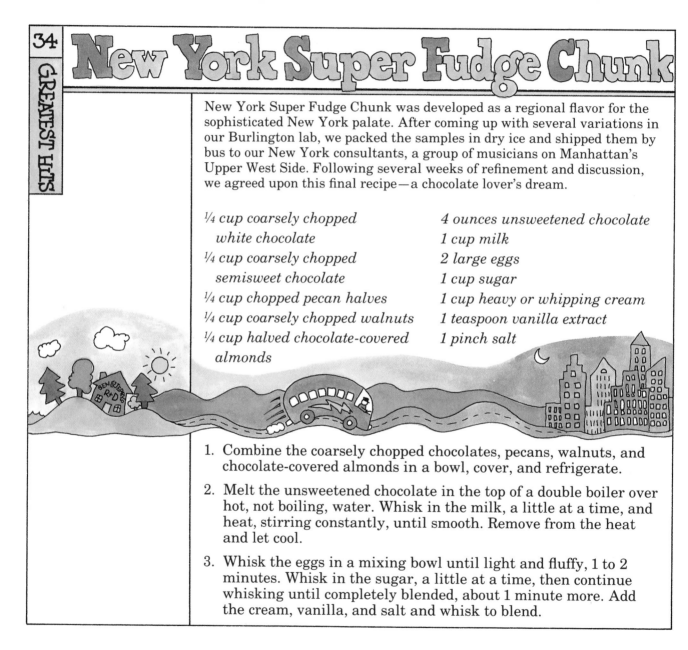

1. Combine the coarsely chopped chocolates, pecans, walnuts, and chocolate-covered almonds in a bowl, cover, and refrigerate.

2. Melt the unsweetened chocolate in the top of a double boiler over hot, not boiling, water. Whisk in the milk, a little at a time, and heat, stirring constantly, until smooth. Remove from the heat and let cool.

3. Whisk the eggs in a mixing bowl until light and fluffy, 1 to 2 minutes. Whisk in the sugar, a little at a time, then continue whisking until completely blended, about 1 minute more. Add the cream, vanilla, and salt and whisk to blend.

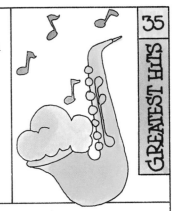
4. Pour the chocolate mixture into the cream mixture and blend. Cover and refrigerate until cold, about 1 to 3 hours, depending on your refrigerator.

5. Transfer the cream mixture to an ice cream maker and freeze following the manufacturer's instructions.

6. After the ice cream stiffens (about 2 minutes before it is done), add the chocolates and nuts, then continue freezing until the ice cream is ready.

Makes generous 1 quart

French Vanilla

A good vanilla ice cream is the measure of all ice creams. We like ours rich, creamy, and easy to make.

2 large eggs	*1 cup milk*
¾ cup sugar	*2 teaspoons vanilla extract*
2 cups heavy or whipping cream	

1. Whisk the eggs in a mixing bowl until light and fluffy, 1 to 2 minutes. Whisk in the sugar, a little at a time, then continue whisking until completely blended, about 1 minute more. Pour in the cream, milk, and vanilla and whisk to blend.

2. Transfer the mixture to an ice cream maker and freeze following the manufacturer's instructions.

Makes 1 quart

Butter Pecan

When buying nuts, look for the freshest you can find, and to keep them fresh, store them in an airtight container in the freezer.

It's important that the pecans in Butter Pecan Ice Cream be as crisp as possible. When sautéed in butter, they can go from crisp to overcooked and soggy very quickly, so keep an eye on them.

Salt is sometimes considered an optional ingredient, but for Butter Pecan Ice Cream, it is a key ingredient. The slightly salty taste is essential to the success of the flavor.

½ cup (1 stick) butter
1 cup pecan halves
½ teaspoon salt
2 large eggs

¾ cup sugar
2 cups heavy or whipping cream
1 cup milk

1. Melt the butter in a heavy skillet over a low heat. Add the pecans and salt and sauté, stirring constantly, until the pecans start to turn brown. Drain the butter into a small bowl and transfer the pecans to another bowl and let cool.

2. Whisk the eggs in a mixing bowl until light and fluffy, 1 to 2 minutes. Whisk the sugar, a little at a time, then continue whisking until completely blended, about 1 minute more. Pour in the cream and milk and whisk to blend. Add the melted butter and blend.

3. Transfer the mixture to an ice cream maker and freeze following the manufacturer's instructions.

4. After the ice cream stiffens (about 2 minutes before it is done), add the pecans, then continue freezing until the ice cream is ready.

Makes generous 1 quart

Dastardly Mash

½ cup raisins
1 cup water
½ cup pecan halves
½ cup roasted salted
  whole almonds
½ cup semisweet chocolate chips
2 ounces unsweetened chocolate

⅓ cup unsweetened cocoa powder
1½ cups milk
1 cup sugar
2 large eggs
1 cup heavy or whipping cream
1 teaspoon vanilla extract

1. Soak the raisins in 1 cup water overnight in the refrigerator.

2. The next day, drain the raisins and combine the raisins, pecans, almonds, and chocolate chips in a bowl. Cover and refrigerate.

3. Melt the unsweetened chocolate in the top of a double boiler over hot, not boiling, water. Gradually whisk in the cocoa and heat, stirring constantly, until smooth. (The chocolate may "seize" or clump together. Don't worry, the milk will dissolve it.) Whisk in the milk, a little at a time, and heat until blended. Remove and let cool.

4. Whisk the eggs in a mixing bowl until light and fluffy, 1 to 2 minutes. Whisk in the sugar, a little at a time, then continue whisking until completely blended, about 1 minute more. Pour in the cream and vanilla extract and whisk to blend.

5. Pour the chocolate mixture into the cream mixture and blend. Cover and refrigerate until cold, about 1 to 3 hours, depending on your refrigerator.

6. Transfer the mixture to an ice cream maker and freeze following the manufacturer's instructions.

7. After the ice cream stiffens (about 2 minutes before it is done), add the raisin mixture, then continue freezing until the ice cream is ready.

Makes generous 1 quart

Jerry says:
Fred and Cleo Alter of the Shoreham Inn in Shoreham, Vermont, came up with the name Dastardly Mash back in the days when Ben was still driving the delivery route in his old square-back VW. When he got back to the store, we began experimenting.

Although Ben hates raisins in his ice cream, we put them in anyway. But it turned out a lot of other people didn't like them either, and we got a lot of complaints.

"Dastardly Mash is a nice ice cream," they said, "but it has too many raisins in it." So we cut down on the raisins. Then we got some more letters. These said, "Dastardly Mash is a nice ice cream, but it doesn't have enough raisins in it." We've since learned the fine art of compromise.

Fresh Georgia Peach

When we first decided to try peach ice cream, we consulted one of Georgia's peach specialists, Dr. Stephen Myers. He invited us down to inspect the orchards.

We arrived at Dickey Farms, our mix in hand, ready to make a test batch. After debating the merits of peeled versus unpeeled peaches, we made a perfect batch with one pound of unpeeled Blake peaches. We then ordered forty tons of fruit—enough to fill two trailer trucks—and had them shipped to Washington, D.C. for pitting and defuzzing.

The following day, they arrived at our plant in Vermont, and we made peach ice cream nonstop for the next four days until we had 172 tons.

Since peach is a seasonal fruit, we only go through this production number once a year.

The best way to capture the elusive flavor of summertime. We prefer small peaches because they have more flavor and less water than the larger ones.

2 cups finely chopped ripe peaches, peeled if you prefer
1¼ cups sugar
Juice of ½ lemon

2 large eggs
2 cups heavy or whipping cream
1 cup milk

1. Combine the peaches, ½ cup of the sugar, and the lemon juice in a bowl. Cover and refrigerate for 2 hours, stirring the mixture every 30 minutes.

2. Remove the peaches from the refrigerator and drain the juice into another bowl. Return the peaches to the refrigerator.

3. Whisk the eggs in a mixing bowl until light and fluffy, 1 to 2 minutes. Whisk in the remaining ¾ cup sugar, a little at a time, then continue whisking until completely blended, about 1 minute more. Pour in the cream and milk and whisk to blend. Add the peach juice and blend.

4. Transfer the mixture to an ice cream maker and freeze following the manufacturer's instructions.

5. After the ice cream stiffens (about 2 minutes before it is done), add the peaches, then continue freezing until the ice cream is ready.

Makes generous 1 quart

Raspberry

Compared to other fresh fruit, fresh raspberries are intensely flavorful and very tart, so to make ice cream you need less fruit and more sugar.

1 pint fresh raspberries
1½ cups sugar
Juice of ½ lemon

2 large eggs
2 cups heavy or whipping cream
1 cup milk

1. Toss the raspberries, ¾ cup of the sugar, and the lemon juice together in a bowl. Cover and refrigerate for 2 hours, stirring every 30 minutes.

2. Whisk the eggs in a mixing bowl until light and fluffy, 1 to 2 minutes. Whisk in the remaining ¾ cup sugar, a little at a time, then continue whisking until completely blended, about 1 minute more. Pour in the heavy cream and milk and whisk to blend.

3. Drain the juice from the raspberries into the cream mixture and blend. Mash the raspberries until puréed and stir them into the cream mixture.

4. Transfer the mixture to an ice cream maker and freeze following the manufacturer's instructions.

Makes generous 1 quart

Note: If you prefer a chunkier raspberry ice cream, return the raspberries to the refrigerator after pouring off the juice. After the ice cream stiffens (about 2 minutes before it is done), add the whole raspberries, then continue freezing until the ice cream is ready.

Mocha Swiss Chocolate Almond

MORE COFFEE WOULD BE PERFECT

Mmm, MORE CHOCOLATE WOULD BE DIVINE

Making a mocha ice cream that satisfies everyone is an elusive goal. In half of our mail, people say they want more chocolate flavor; the other half wants more coffee flavor. We've considered matching up the writers and sending them each other's letters.

2 large eggs

¾ cup sugar

4 teaspoons unsweetened cocoa powder

2 tablespoons good-quality freeze-dried coffee

2 cups heavy or whipping cream

1 cup milk

1 cup chocolate-covered almonds

1. Whisk the eggs in a mixing bowl until light and fluffy, 1 to 2 minutes. Whisk in the sugar, a little at a time, then continue whisking until completely blended, about 1 minute more. Add the cocoa and coffee and whisk to blend. Whisk in the cream and milk thoroughly.

2. Transfer the mixture to an ice cream maker and freeze following the manufacturer's instructions.

3. After the ice cream stiffens (about 2 minutes before it is done), add the almonds, then continue freezing until the ice cream is ready.

Makes generous 1 quart

Oreo Mint

We've been making Oreo Mint ever since we opened our first store in the gas station. It was our top-selling flavor for a long time and was only recently nudged out of first place by the inimitable Heath Bar Crunch.

⅔ cup coarsely chopped
   Oreo cookies
2 large eggs
¾ cup sugar

2 cups heavy or whipping cream
1 cup milk
2 teaspoons peppermint extract

1. Place the cookies in a bowl, cover, and refrigerate.

2. Whisk the eggs in a mixing bowl until light and fluffy, 1 to 2 minutes. Whisk in the sugar, a little at a time, then continue whisking until completely blended, about 1 minute more. Pour in the cream and milk and whisk to blend. Add the peppermint extract and blend again.

3. Transfer the mixture to an ice cream maker and freeze following the manufacturer's instructions.

4. After the ice cream stiffens (about 2 minutes before it is done), add the chopped cookies, then continue freezing until the ice cream is ready.

   Makes generous 1 quart

HOME OF OREO MINT

BEN & JERRY'S ICE CRE

BEN & JERRY'S HOMEMADE

Oreo® is a registered trademark of Nabisco Brands, Inc.

Cherry Garcia™

A couple of Dead Heads in Maine sent us a postcard with a name for a new flavor. They left the recipe up to us. We got to work with some fresh bing cherries and threw in the chocolate flakes as a last minute inspiration. At last report, both Jerry Garcia and his wife Carolyn are crazy about it.

¼ cup shaved plain chocolate
   (we prefer Hershey's Special
   Dark Chocolate candy bars)

¼ cup fresh Bing cherries, halved
   and pitted (you may use
   canned cherries, but be sure
   to drain the syrup)

2 large eggs

¾ cup sugar

2 cups heavy or whipping cream

1 cup milk

1. Place the shaved chocolate flakes and the cherries in separate bowls. Cover and refrigerate.

2. Whisk the eggs in a mixing bowl until light and fluffy, 1 to 2 minutes. Whisk in the sugar, a little at a time, then continue whisking until completely blended, about 1 minute more. Pour in the cream and milk and whisk to blend.

3. Transfer the mixture to an ice cream maker and freeze following the manufacturer's instructions.

4. After the ice cream stiffens (about 2 minutes before it is done), add the chocolate and the cherries, then continue freezing until the ice cream is ready.

Makes grateful 1 quart

How to Shave a Chocolate Bar
Easy. Place the chocolate in the freezer until it is very hard. Then shave over a bowl using a cheese grater.

POSTCARD

Dear Bent Jerry,
We thought of a name for a new flavor of your ice cream. Get this! Cherry Garcia. What do ya think? It can be just a ...cherries &

Greetings From MAIN

Ben...

Chocolate ice creams

The love of chocolate lies somewhere between obsession and fanaticism. But true chocoholics are devout connoisseurs as well. Our basic chocolate ice cream recipes — designed to satisfy the most demanding — are about as rich as you will find anywhere. If you like both chocolate and complex texture, try our Dastardly Mash and New York Superfudge Chunk from the Greatest Hits list.

Ben's Chocolate

Ben's Chocolate Ice Cream is about as rich as they come. The pinch of salt helps to bring out the chocolate flavor.

4 ounces unsweetened chocolate	*1 cup heavy or whipping cream*
1 cup milk	*1 teaspoon vanilla extract*
2 large eggs	*1 pinch salt*
1 cup sugar	

1. Melt the unsweetened chocolate in the top of a double boiler over hot, not boiling, water. Gradually whisk in the milk and heat, stirring constantly, until smooth. Remove from the heat and let cool.

2. Whisk the eggs in a mixing bowl until light and fluffy, 1 to 2 minutes. Whisk in the sugar, a little at a time, then continue whisking until completely blended, about 1 minute more. Add the cream, vanilla, and salt and whisk to blend.

3. Pour the chocolate mixture into the cream mixture and blend. Cover and refrigerate until cold, about 1 to 3 hours, depending on your refrigerator.

4. Transfer the mixture to an ice cream maker and freeze following the manufacturer's instructions.

Makes 1 quart

VARIATION: Chocolate Almond

Add 1 cup roasted whole almonds (salted or unsalted) after the ice cream stiffens (about 2 minutes before it is done), then continue freezing until the ice cream is ready.

Jerry's Chocolate

The combination of cocoa powder and unsweetened chocolate creates an ice cream with a more complex texture. Jerry refers to this as "mouthfeel."

2 ounces unsweetened chocolate	1 cup sugar
⅓ cup unsweetened cocoa powder	1 cup heavy or whipping cream
1½ cups milk	1 teaspoon vanilla extract
2 large eggs	

1. Melt the unsweetened chocolate in the top of a double boiler over hot, not boiling, water. Gradually whisk in the cocoa and heat, stirring constantly, until smooth. (The chocolate may "seize" or clump together. Don't worry, the milk will dissolve it.) Whisk in the milk, a little at a time, and heat until completely blended. Remove from the heat and let cool.

2. Whisk the eggs in a mixing bowl until light and fluffy, 1 to 2 minutes. Whisk in the sugar, a little at a time, then continue whisking until completely blended, about 1 minute more. Pour in the cream and vanilla and whisk to blend.

3. Pour the chocolate mixture into the cream mixture and blend. Cover and refrigerate until cold, about 1 to 3 hours, depending on your refrigerator.

4. Transfer the mixture to an ice cream maker and freeze following the manufacturer's instructions.

Makes 1 quart

"mouthfeel"

VARIATION: Chocolate Chocolate Chip

Add ¾ cup semisweet chocolate chips after the ice cream stiffens (about 2 minutes before it is done), then continue freezing until the ice cream is ready.

This rich, fully textured ice cream is a chocoholic's delight. Some of our friends take it a step further and serve it with hot fudge sauce.

Light Chocolate

Light Chocolate Ice Cream is slightly less rich than Ben's or Jerry's Chocolate. It acts as a good background for other flavors, especially the more subtle ones. Try it when adding cinnamon, carob chips, malt powder, or peppermint extract (variations follow). It also provides a good showcase for peanut butter and bananas.

1 ounce unsweetened chocolate
¼ cup unsweetened cocoa powder
1½ cups milk
2 large eggs

¾ cup sugar
1 cup heavy or whipping cream
1 teaspoon vanilla extract

1. Melt the unsweetened chocolate in the top of a double boiler over hot, not boiling, water. Gradually whisk in the cocoa and heat, stirring constantly, until smooth. (The chocolate may "seize" or clump together. Don't worry, the milk will dissolve it.) Whisk in the milk, a little at a time, and heat until completely blended. Remove from the heat and let cool.

2. Whisk the eggs in a mixing bowl until light and fluffy, 1 to 2 minutes. Whisk in the sugar, a little at a time, then continue whisking until completely blended, about 1 minute more. Pour in the cream and vanilla and whisk to blend.

3. Pour the chocolate mixture into the cream mixture and blend. Cover and refrigerate until cold, about 1 to 3 hours, depending on your refrigerator.

4. Transfer the mixture to an ice cream maker and freeze following the manufacturer's instructions.

Makes 1 quart

VARIATIONS: Chocolate Cinnamon

Whisk 1 tablespoon ground cinnamon into the mixture just before transferring it to the ice cream maker.

Chocolate Cinnamon Carob

Prepare the Chocolate Cinnamon Ice Cream as directed. After the ice cream stiffens (about 2 minutes before it is done), add ¾ cup carob chips, then continue freezing until the ice cream is ready.

Chocolate Malt

Whisk ⅓ cup malt powder into the mixture just before transferring it to the ice cream maker.

Chocolate Mint

Whisk 1 teaspoon peppermint extract into the mixture just before transferring it to the ice cream maker.

Chocolate Peanut Butter

Just before transferring the mixture to the ice cream maker, pour about 1 cup of it into a separate bowl. Add ½ cup smooth peanut butter and whisk until completely blended. Return to the remaining mixture and blend.

VARIATIONS: Light Chocolate Banana

Mash 2 overripe bananas and the juice of 1 lemon together in a bowl, then whisk until smooth. After the ice cream stiffens (about 2 minutes before it is done), add the banana mixture, then continue freezing until the ice cream is ready.

Light Chocolate Nutty Fudge Chunk

Add ¾ cup coarsely chopped chocolate fudge and roasted salted whole almonds after the ice cream stiffens (about 2 minutes before it is done), then continue freezing until the ice cream is ready.

Mandarin Chocolate

Thaw ½ cup frozen orange juice concentrate and whisk it into the mixture just before transferring it to the ice cream maker.

Fruit FLAVORS

Although absolutely the best fruit ice cream is made with fresh, hand-picked produce, it is possible to use frozen, and sometimes, canned fruit. We like to purée our fruit by mashing it with an old-fashioned potato masher.

SWEETENING the Fruit

Extra sugar is usually required when making fruit-flavored ice creams, but the proportion varies, depending on the natural sweetness of each fruit. Bananas are especially sweet and require no additional sugar. Raspberries, on the other hand, are extremely tart and require the greatest amount of sugar.

Fruit

	PROPORTION OF Fruit to SUGAR
Bananas	no added sugar
Apples	7 to 1
Strawberries	4 to 1
Peaches	4 to 1
Plums	4 to 1
Pineapple	4 to 1
Apricots	3 to 1
Blackberries	3 to 1
Cherries	3 to 1
Raspberries	2 to 1

Jerry Guesses:

Papaya	3 to 1
Mango	4 to 1
Pear	4 to 1

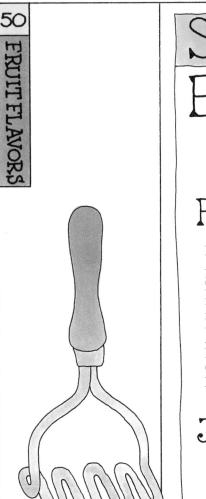

When mashing fresh fruit, try using a potato masher. It's simple, basic, and works every time.

 Apple Strawberry

We prefer McIntosh apples, but any crispy apple will do.

*1 pint fresh strawberries, hulled
  and sliced*
Juice of ½ lemon
Sweet Cream Base (pages 28–29)

*½ cup apple cider jelly
  (see page 64)*
1 cup peeled diced apples

1. Combine the strawberries and half the lemon juice in a bowl.
    Cover and refrigerate at least 1 hour.

2. Prepare the Sweet Cream Base. Drain the juice from the straw-
    berries into the base, add the apple jelly, and blend. Return the
    strawberries to the refrigerator.

3. Toss the apples and remaining lemon juice together in a separ-
    ate bowl. Cover and refrigerate.

4. Transfer the base to an ice cream maker and freeze following the
    manufacturer's instructions.

5. After the ice cream stiffens (about 2 minutes before it is done),
    add the strawberries and apples, then continue freezing until the
    ice cream is ready.

Makes generous 1 quart

Banana

We've tried making this ice cream with frozen bananas, frozen sliced bananas, and banana purée, but nothing works as well as overripe bananas—the more brown spots the better.

Sweet Cream Base (pages 28–29)   *Juice of 1 lemon*
2 overripe bananas

1. Prepare the Sweet Cream Base. Transfer to an ice cream maker and freeze following the manufacturer's directions.

2. Mash the bananas and lemon juice together in a bowl, then whisk until smooth.

3. After the ice cream stiffens (about 2 minutes before it is done), add the banana mixture, then continue freezing until the ice cream is ready.

Makes generous 1 quart

VARIATIONS: Banana Fudge Chunk

Stir 1 cup cold coarsely chopped chocolate fudge into the banana mixture before adding to the ice cream.

Banana Carob-Chip

Stir ½ cup carob chips into the banana mixture before adding it to the ice cream.

Banana Cinnamon Rum

Whisk 2 tablespoons ground cinnamon and 2 tablespoons rum, preferably dark, into the cream base just before transferring to the ice cream maker. Complete the recipe as directed.

Banana Strawberry

FRUIT FLAVORS

Try this flavor when fresh strawberries are not available.

1 overripe medium banana
⅔ cup frozen strawberries in
  syrup, thawed

Juice of ¼ lemon
Sweet Cream Base (pages 28–29)

1. Mash the banana in a bowl. Drain the strawberries and add the syrup and lemon juice to the banana. Whisk until smooth.

2. Prepare the Sweet Cream Base. Add the banana mixture and blend.

3. Transfer the mixture to an ice cream maker and freeze following the manufacturer's instructions.

4. After the ice cream stiffens (about 2 minutes before it is done), add the strawberries, then continue freezing until the ice cream is ready.

Makes generous 1 quart

Strawberry

Use the freshest strawberries possible for this ice cream. We've been told that the early morning is the best time to pick strawberries because they are still cool.

1 pint fresh strawberries,
hulled and sliced
⅓ cup sugar

Juice of ½ lemon
Sweet Cream Base (pages 28–29)

1. Combine the strawberries, sugar, and lemon juice in a mixing bowl. Cover and refrigerate at least 1 hour.

2. Prepare the Sweet Cream Base. Mash the strawberries to a purée and stir into the cream base.

3. Transfer the mixture to an ice cream maker and freeze following the manufacturer's instructions.

Makes generous 1 quart

Note: For a chunkier ice cream, drain the juice from the strawberries and whisk it into the cream base just before transferring it to the ice cream maker. After the ice cream stiffens (about 2 minutes before it is done), add the mashed strawberries, then continue freezing until the ice cream is ready.

Cantaloupe

This is one of Jerry's favorite flavors, but we never figured out how to make it in large batches. It's sold only in our downtown store.

1 large or 2 small cantaloupes,
  very ripe

Juice of 1 lemon
Sweet Cream Base (pages 28–29)

1. Cut the cantaloupe in half and clean out the seeds. Scoop the fruit into a mixing bowl, add the lemon juice, and mash until the fruit is puréed. Drain the juice into another bowl and reserve. Cover the melon purée and refrigerate.

2. Prepare the Sweet Cream Base and whisk in the fruit juice.

3. Transfer the mixture to an ice cream maker and freeze following the manufacturer's instructions.

4. After the ice cream stiffens (about 2 minutes before it is done), add the cantaloupe. If more juice has accumulated, do not pour it in because it will water down the ice cream. Continue freezing until the ice cream is ready.

Makes generous 1 quart

VARIATION: Coconut Cantaloupe

Use half the amount of cantaloupe and lemon juice asked for in step 1. Add 1 cup coconut cream, such as Coco Lopez, to the Sweet Cream Base in step 2. Complete the recipe as directed.

Orange Cream Dream

This recipe for Orange Cream Dream is easy to make and very refreshing. It brings back memories of waiting for the ice cream man on warm summer evenings.

Sweet Cream Base (pages 28–29)   *2 teaspoons vanilla extract*
⅓ cup frozen orange juice
*   concentrate, thawed*

1. Prepare the Sweet Cream Base. Add the juice concentrate and vanilla extract and blend.

2. Transfer the mixture to an ice cream maker and freeze following the manufacturer's instructions.

Makes generous 1 quart

Kiwi Ice Cream

Kiwi Ice Cream is one of our more exotic, subtle flavors for the true connoisseur.

6 ripe kiwis   *2 large eggs*
1 cup plus 2 tablespoons sugar   *2 cups heavy or whipping cream*

1. Peel the kiwis and mash them in a bowl until puréed. Stir 2 tablespoons sugar into the fruit, cover, and refrigerate 1 hour.

2. Whisk the eggs in a mixing bowl until light and fluffy, 1 to 2 minutes. Whisk in 1 cup sugar, a little at a time, then continue

whisking until completely blended, about 1 minute more. Pour in the cream and whisk to blend. Stir in the kiwis.

3. Transfer the mixture to an ice cream maker and freeze following the manufacturer's instructions.

Makes 1 quart

Plum Ice Cream

If you really like plums, this is the flavor to try. The recipe works well with any variety of plum, as long as it's fresh.

1 cup chopped, peeled very
  ripe plums

¼ cup sugar
Sweet Cream Base (pages 28–29)

1. Combine the plums and sugar in a bowl and mash until puréed. Cover and refrigerate 1 hour.

2. Prepare the Sweet Cream Base. Drain the juice from the plums into the cream base and blend. Return the plum purée to the refrigerator.

3. Transfer the mixture to an ice cream maker and freeze following the manufacturer's instructions.

4. After the ice cream stiffens (about 2 minutes before it is done), add the plum purée, then continue freezing until the ice cream is ready.

Makes generous 1 quart

Pumpkin

One Halloween, we tried to make pumpkin ice cream with fresh pumpkins. It was very messy and complicated and didn't taste nearly as good as this simple recipe using canned pumpkin.

Sweet Cream Base (pages 28–29)
1 cup unsweetened canned
  pumpkin

1 teaspoon ground or freshly
  grated nutmeg
1 teaspoon ground cinnamon

1. Prepare the Sweet Cream Base. Pour about 1 cup of the cream base into another bowl, add the pumpkin, nutmeg, and cinnamon, and stir until blended. Return the pumpkin mixture to the remaining cream base and blend.

2. Transfer the mixture to an ice cream maker and freeze following the manufacturer's instructions.

Makes generous 1 quart

Strawberry Coconut

1 large egg
½ cup sugar
2 cups heavy or whipping cream
1 cup frozen strawberries
  in syrup, thawed

1 can (15 ounces) coconut cream,
  such as Coco Lopez
Juice of ¼ lemon

1. Whisk the first 3 ingredients together. Drain the strawberries and add the syrup, coconut cream, and lemon juice to the cream base. Whisk to blend.

2. Transfer the mixture to an ice cream maker and freeze following the manufacturer's instructions.

3. After the ice cream stiffens (about 2 minutes before it is done), add the strawberries, then continue freezing until the ice cream is ready.

Makes generous 1 quart

Wild Blueberry

We recommend using freshly picked wild blueberries. Cultivated blueberries don't seem to have much taste.

1 pint small wild blueberries
½ cup sugar

Juice of ½ lemon
Sweet Cream Base (pages 28–29)

1. Toss the blueberries, sugar, and lemon juice together in a mixing bowl. Cover and refrigerate 2 hours, stirring every 30 minutes.

2. Prepare the Sweet Cream Base. Drain the juice from the blueberries into the cream base and blend. Mash the blueberries until puréed and stir into the cream base.

3. Transfer the mixture to an ice cream maker and freeze following the manufacturer's instructions.

Makes generous 1 quart

DOWNTOWN Specials

ur piano-playing friend, Don Rose, always insisted that the word "ambience" was too elegant to describe what you might find in our original downtown store. The interior decoration was eclectic at best, and our antique White Mountain ice cream freezer was definitely funky, but our customers — the local Burlington downtown crowd — defied description, as did their special requests. Nevertheless, they were always cheerful and willing and eager to sample new flavors and inspire us to greater heights.

Almond Delight

Sweet Cream Base (pages 28–29)
2 teaspoons almond extract

⅔ cup coarsely chopped roasted almonds (lightly salted or unsalted)

1. Prepare the Sweet Cream Base. Add the almond extract and whisk to blend.

2. Transfer the mixture to an ice cream maker and freeze following the manufacturer's instructions.

3. After the ice cream stiffens (about 2 minutes before it is done), add the almonds, then continue freezing until the ice cream is ready.

Makes generous 1 quart

Banana Peanut Butter

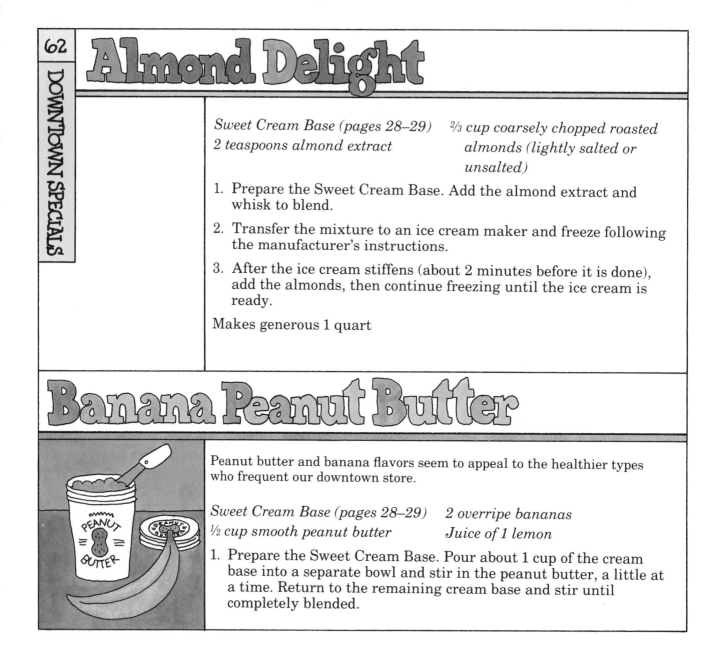

Peanut butter and banana flavors seem to appeal to the healthier types who frequent our downtown store.

Sweet Cream Base (pages 28–29)
½ cup smooth peanut butter

2 overripe bananas
Juice of 1 lemon

1. Prepare the Sweet Cream Base. Pour about 1 cup of the cream base into a separate bowl and stir in the peanut butter, a little at a time. Return to the remaining cream base and stir until completely blended.

2. Transfer the mixture to an ice cream maker and freeze following the manufacturer's instructions.

3. Mash the bananas in a bowl, add the lemon juice, and whisk until smooth.

4. After the ice cream stiffens (about 2 minutes before it is done), add the banana mixture, then continue freezing until the ice cream is ready.

Makes generous 1 quart

Chocolate Chip Cookie Dough

The idea of using raw dough may not sound very appealing, but as those who have trouble keeping their fingers out of the cookie dough know, the taste is terrific.

½ recipe (1½ cups) raw Giant Chocolate Chip Cookie Dough (page 98)

Sweet Cream Base (pages 28–29) 2 teaspoons vanilla extract

1. Chop the cookie dough into bite-size pieces, place in a bowl, cover, and freeze.

2. Prepare the Sweet Cream Base. Add the vanilla extract and blend.

3. Transfer the mixture to an ice cream maker and freeze following the manufacturer's instructions.

4. When the ice cream is quite stiff (about 1 minute before it is done), add the chopped cookie dough. Be sure to wait until the very last moment, otherwise the dough will get sticky and unmanageable. Continue freezing until the ice cream is ready.

Makes generous 1 quart

DOWNTOWN SPECIALS

Honey Apple Raisin Walnut

We use apple cider jelly made at the Cold Hollow Cider Mill, just up the road from our Waterbury plant. If you can't find apple cider jelly, try using apple jelly.

⅓ cup raisins

1 cup water

2 large eggs

½ cup light honey

2 cups heavy or whipping cream

1 cup milk

¼ cup apple cider jelly

⅓ cup coarsely chopped walnuts

1. Soak the raisins in 1 cup water overnight in the refrigerator.

2. The next day, whisk the eggs in a mixing bowl until light and fluffy, 1 to 2 minutes. Add the honey and whisk until completely blended. Pour in the cream and milk and whisk to blend.

3. Pour about ½ cup of the cream mixture into a separate bowl, add the jelly, and mix until smooth. Return to the remaining cream mixture and blend.

4. Transfer the mixture to an ice cream maker and freeze following the manufacturer's instructions.

5. Drain the raisins. After the ice cream stiffens (about 2 minutes before it is done), mix the raisins and walnuts together and add them to the ice cream. Continue freezing until the ice cream is ready.

Makes generous 1 quart

**The Cold Hollow
Cider Mill**

There are only two cider mills in the country that produce pure apple cider jelly, and one of them is just several miles north of our plant in Waterbury Center, where Eric and Francine Chittenden run the Cold Hollow Cider Mill. This is the best place to get apple cider jelly and apple cider syrup. They also sell all grades of pure Vermont Amber Maple Syrup and will ship it anywhere. Call them at (800) 527-5237 or stop by to watch them make fresh apple cider.

Cappuccino

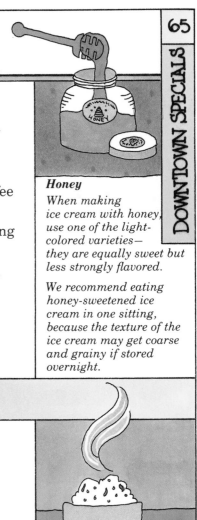

Serve with freshly whipped cream.

Sweet Cream Base (pages 28–29)   *1 tablespoon ground cinnamon*
3½ tablespoons good-quality
* freeze-dried coffee*

1. Prepare the Sweet Cream Base. Add 2½ tablespoons of the coffee and the cinnamon and blend.

2. Transfer the mixture to an ice cream maker and freeze following the manufacturer's instructions.

3. After the ice cream stiffens (about 2 minutes before it is done), add the remaining 1 tablespoon coffee, then continue freezing until the ice cream is ready.

Makes 1 quart

Honey
*When making
ice cream with honey,
use one of the light-
colored varieties—
they are equally sweet but
less strongly flavored.*

*We recommend eating
honey-sweetened ice
cream in one sitting,
because the texture of the
ice cream may get coarse
and grainy if stored
overnight.*

VARIATION: Cappuccino Chip

Add ½ cup chocolate chips with the last tablespoon of coffee after the ice cream stiffens (about 2 minutes before it is done).

Coffee

Coffee Ice Cream can also be made with coffee concentrate that has been prepared at least one day ahead of time. Dan Cox of Green Mountain Roasters recommends using either a full-bodied blend of coffee such as Viennese Roast or a very flavorful Sumatran blend such as Sumatra-Kona.

2 large eggs
¾ cup plus 2 tablespoons sugar
2 cups heavy or whipping cream

1 cup milk
3 tablespoons good-quality
freeze-dried coffee

1. Whisk the eggs in a mixing bowl until light and fluffy, 1 to 2 minutes. Whisk in the sugar, a little at a time, then continue whisking until completely blended, about 1 minute more. Add the cream, milk, and 2 tablespoons of the coffee and whisk to blend.

2. Transfer the mixture to an ice cream maker and freeze following the manufacturer's instructions.

3. After the ice cream stiffens (about 2 minutes before it is done), add the remaining 1 tablespoon coffee, then continue freezing until the ice cream is ready.

Makes 1 quart

Making Coffee Concentrate

To prepare coffee concentrate, you will need a coffee toddy, 1 pound medium to fine ground coffee, and ½ gallon cold water. Set the toddy over an empty jar, place the coffee in the filter, and pour the water over it. Let the coffee drip overnight. This makes 5 ounces of concentrate. Use only 4½ teaspoons for each batch of ice cream.

VARIATION: Coffee Almond Swirl

Add ¾ cup roasted whole almonds (salted or unsalted) after the ice cream stiffens (about 2 minutes before it is done), then continue freezing until the ice cream is ready. Remove the dasher and fold in 1 cup cold fudge sauce with a spatula.

Coconut

Be sure to discard the waxy disk at the bottom of the can of coconut cream. It's edible, but it doesn't combine well with the cream base.

Sweet Cream Base 1 (page 28)   *1 can (15 ounces) coconut cream, such as Coco Lopez*

1. Prepare the Sweet Cream Base. Add the coconut cream and blend.
2. Transfer the mixture to an ice cream maker and freeze following the manufacturer's instructions.

Makes generous 1 quart

VARIATIONS: Coconut Almond

Add ¾ cup roasted whole almonds (salted or unsalted) after the ice cream stiffens (about 2 minutes before it is done), then continue freezing until the ice cream is ready.

Coconut Chip

Add ¾ cup semisweet chocolate chips after the ice cream stiffens (about 2 minutes before it is done), then continue freezing until the ice cream is ready.

Coconut Rum

Whisk 2 tablespoons rum, preferably dark, into the cream mixture before transferring it to the ice cream maker. Complete the recipe as directed.

Chocolate Fudge Pecan

Ben's Chocolate Ice Cream
  (page 44)   *1 cup fudge sauce, cold*
¾ cup pecan halves

1. Prepare Ben's Chocolate Ice Cream. After the ice cream stiffens (about 2 minutes before it is done), add the pecans, then continue freezing until the ice cream is ready.

2. Remove the dasher and fold in the fudge sauce with a spatula.

Makes generous 1 quart

Kahlúa Amaretto

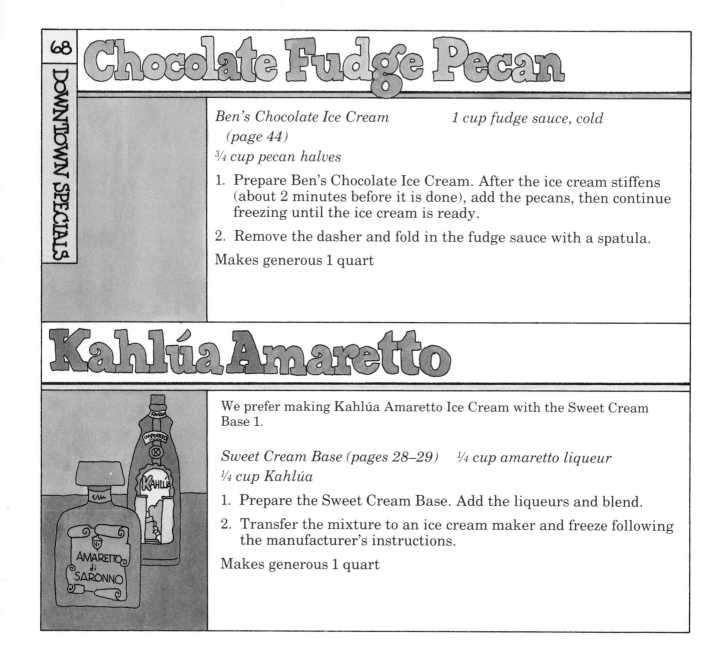

We prefer making Kahlúa Amaretto Ice Cream with the Sweet Cream Base 1.

Sweet Cream Base (pages 28–29)   *¼ cup amaretto liqueur*
¼ cup Kahlúa

1. Prepare the Sweet Cream Base. Add the liqueurs and blend.

2. Transfer the mixture to an ice cream maker and freeze following the manufacturer's instructions.

Makes generous 1 quart

Kahlúa Almond Fudge

When folding in fudge sauce, work as quickly as possible to keep the fudge from blending in and making chocolate ice cream.

¾ cup roasted whole almonds
  (salted or unsalted)
1 large egg
⅓ cup sugar

1 cup heavy or whipping cream
½ cup milk
½ cup Kahlúa
1 cup fudge sauce, cold

1. Whisk the first 4 ingredients together. Add the Kahlúa and blend.

2. Transfer the mixture to an ice cream maker and freeze following the manufacturer's instructions.

3. When the ice cream begins to stiffen (about 5 minutes before it is done), add the almonds, then continue freezing until the ice cream is ready.

4. Remove the dasher and fold in the fudge sauce with a spatula.

Makes generous 1 quart

Maple Walnut

Although Maple Walnut Ice Cream is commonly associated with Vermont, it's not a very popular flavor here, which left us wondering who actually liked it. We recently found our answer when we scooped free ice cream at the Vermont Agriculture Day Celebrations in Montpelier. To our surprise, all the state legislators lined up for Maple Walnut Ice Cream and consumed it with great passion.

Sweet Cream Base (pages 28–29)   *½ cup coarsely chopped walnuts*

¼ cup maple syrup, preferably
  grade C

1. Prepare the Sweet Cream Base. Add the maple syrup and stir until blended.

2. Transfer the mixture to an ice cream maker and freeze following the manufacturer's instructions.

3. After the ice cream stiffens (about 2 minutes before it is done), add the walnuts, then continue freezing until the ice cream is ready.

Makes generous 1 quart

The Cold Hollow Maple Syrup Chart

Our friends over at the Cold Hollow Cider Mill sell their maple syrup in these grades:

Fancy/U.S. Grade A (Light Amber)
A clear, light amber syrup with a very delicate taste. It is the first run from the tree and takes longer to boil down.

Grade A/U.S. Grade A (Medium Amber)
Also a clear syrup but slightly darker than fancy and with a stronger maple flavor.

Grade B/U.S. Grade A (Dark Amber)
A dark amber syrup that may be slightly cloudy. The flavor is strong, tending toward caramel.

Grade C and all lower grades
Not sold as a table syrup but rather as a baking sweetener. It is dark and heavy.

Maple Grape Nuts

The healthy types who hang out in our downtown store gave us the inspiration for this flavor.

Sweet Cream Base 1 (page 28) *¾ cup Grape-Nuts*

¼ cup maple syrup, preferably
 Grade C

1. Prepare the Sweet Cream Base. Add the maple syrup and blend.

2. Transfer the mixture to an ice cream maker and freeze following the manufacturer's instructions.

3. After the ice cream stiffens (about 2 minutes before it is done), add the Grape-Nuts, then continue freezing until the ice cream is ready.

Makes generous 1 quart

Post®Grape-Nuts® is manufactured by General Foods Corporation.

Mocha

The coffee tempers the chocolate so the ice cream is not too sweet. This is a very popular flavor.

2 cups heavy or whipping cream
1 cup milk
¾ cup sugar
4 teaspoons unsweetened
  cocoa powder

2 tablespoons good-quality
  freeze-dried coffee
2 large eggs

1. Mix the cream, milk, sugar, cocoa, and coffee in a mixing bowl until blended. Whisk the eggs in another bowl until light yellow. Pour the eggs into the cream mixture and stir until blended.

2. Transfer the mixture to an ice cream maker and freeze following the manufacturer's instructions.

Makes 1 quart

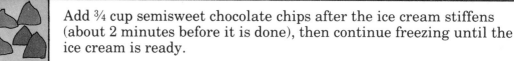

VARIATIONS: Mocha Chip

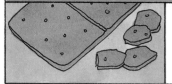

Add ¾ cup semisweet chocolate chips after the ice cream stiffens (about 2 minutes before it is done), then continue freezing until the ice cream is ready.

Chocolate Graham Mocha Supreme

Coarsely chop enough chocolate-covered graham crackers to measure 1 cup and refrigerate. Add the crackers after the ice cream stiffens (about 2 minutes before it is done), then continue freezing until the ice cream is ready.

Mocha Fudge Chunk

About an hour before making the ice cream, chop enough fudge to measure 1 cup and freeze. Add the fudge after the ice cream stiffens (about 2 minutes before it is done), then continue freezing until the ice cream is ready.

Mocha Heath Bar Crunch

About an hour before making the ice cream, coarsely chop 4 original Heath Bars (you should have about 1 cup). Refrigerate in a covered bowl. After the ice cream stiffens (about 2 minutes before it is done), add the Heath Bars, then continue freezing until the ice cream is ready.

Mocha Walnut

Add 1 cup coarsely chopped walnuts after the ice cream stiffens (about 2 minutes before it is done), then continue freezing until the ice cream is ready.

Ben says:
Mocha Walnut is my all-time favorite flavor, but when we packed it in pints, it turned out to be our all-time worst-selling ice cream. Jerry is fond of saying that there's no accounting for personal taste.

Heath® is a registered trademark of L.S. Heath & Sons, Inc.

Peanut Brittle

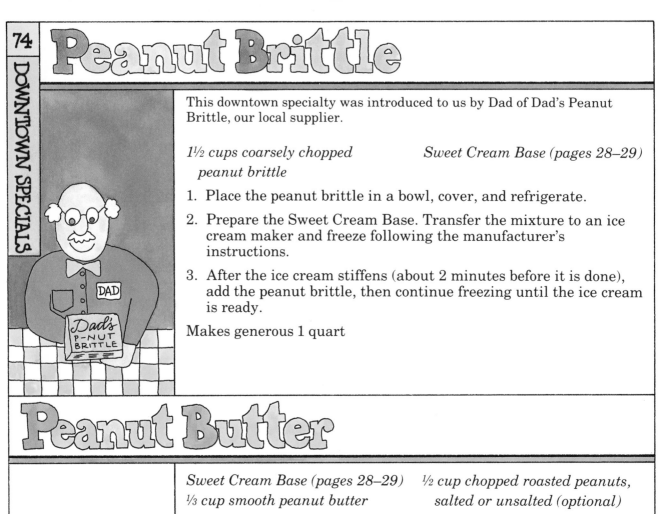

This downtown specialty was introduced to us by Dad of Dad's Peanut Brittle, our local supplier.

1½ cups coarsely chopped peanut brittle

Sweet Cream Base (pages 28–29)

1. Place the peanut brittle in a bowl, cover, and refrigerate.

2. Prepare the Sweet Cream Base. Transfer the mixture to an ice cream maker and freeze following the manufacturer's instructions.

3. After the ice cream stiffens (about 2 minutes before it is done), add the peanut brittle, then continue freezing until the ice cream is ready.

Makes generous 1 quart

Peanut Butter

Sweet Cream Base (pages 28–29)
⅓ cup smooth peanut butter

½ cup chopped roasted peanuts, salted or unsalted (optional)

1. Prepare the Sweet Cream Base. Pour about 1 cup of the cream base into a separate bowl and whisk in the peanut butter, a little at a time. Return the peanut butter mixture to the remaining cream base and stir until well blended.

2. Transfer the mixture to an ice cream maker and freeze following the manufacturer's instructions.

3. If you like a chunky peanut butter ice cream, add the peanuts when the ice cream begins to stiffen (about 5 minutes before it is done), then continue freezing until the ice cream is ready.

Makes generous 1 quart

VARIATIONS: Peanut Butter Chocolate Chip

Leave out the chopped peanuts and add ¾ cup semisweet chocolate chips after the ice cream stiffens (about 2 minutes before it is done), then continue freezing until the ice cream is ready.

There's not much middle ground with Peanut Butter Chocolate Chip. Either you love it or you leave it.

Peanut Butter Fudge Swirl

About 10 minutes before the ice cream is ready, place 1 cup coarsely chopped chocolate fudge in the top of a double boiler and melt over hot, not boiling, water; simmer for 3 to 4 minutes. Remove from the heat and let cool about 5 minutes. Just before the fudge hardens, fold it into the ice cream, then continue freezing until the ice cream is ready.

Egg Nog

Egg Nog Shakes

To make a wonderfully delicious, rich, and creamy egg nog shake, blend a couple of scoops of egg nog ice cream and some milk in a blender. Top with freshly grated nutmeg. This drink is far better than any egg nog you can buy.

Ben says:

Because the recipe calls for eight egg yolks, we've always wondered what to do with the extra egg whites. I put them in a covered bowl and store them in the refrigerator. After a month, I throw them out.

Egg Nog Ice Cream is always very rich and satisfying, but using freshly grated nutmeg and fresh spices will make it even better.

Sweet Cream Base (pages 28–29)
8 large egg yolks
1 teaspoon ground cinnamon
½ teaspoon freshly grated or
* ground nutmeg*
½ teaspoon ground cloves

1. Prepare the Sweet Cream Base.

2. Whisk the egg yolks in another bowl until light yellow. Add the cinnamon, nutmeg, and cloves and blend. Pour the egg yolk mixture into the cream base and stir until blended.

3. Transfer the mixture to an ice cream maker and freeze following the manufacturer's instructions.

Makes generous 1 quart

Vanilla Malt Chip

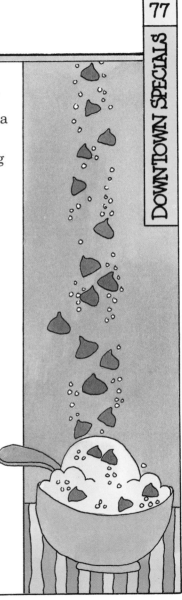

Sweet Cream Base (pages 28–29)
⅓ cup malt powder

2 teaspoons vanilla extract
½ cup semisweet chocolate chips

1. Prepare the Sweet Cream Base. Add the malt powder and vanilla and whisk until blended. Let sit 10 to 15 minutes.

2. Transfer the mixture to an ice cream maker and freeze following the manufacturer's instructions.

3. After the ice cream stiffens (about 2 minutes before it is done), add the chocolate chips, then continue freezing until the ice cream is ready.

Makes generous 1 quart

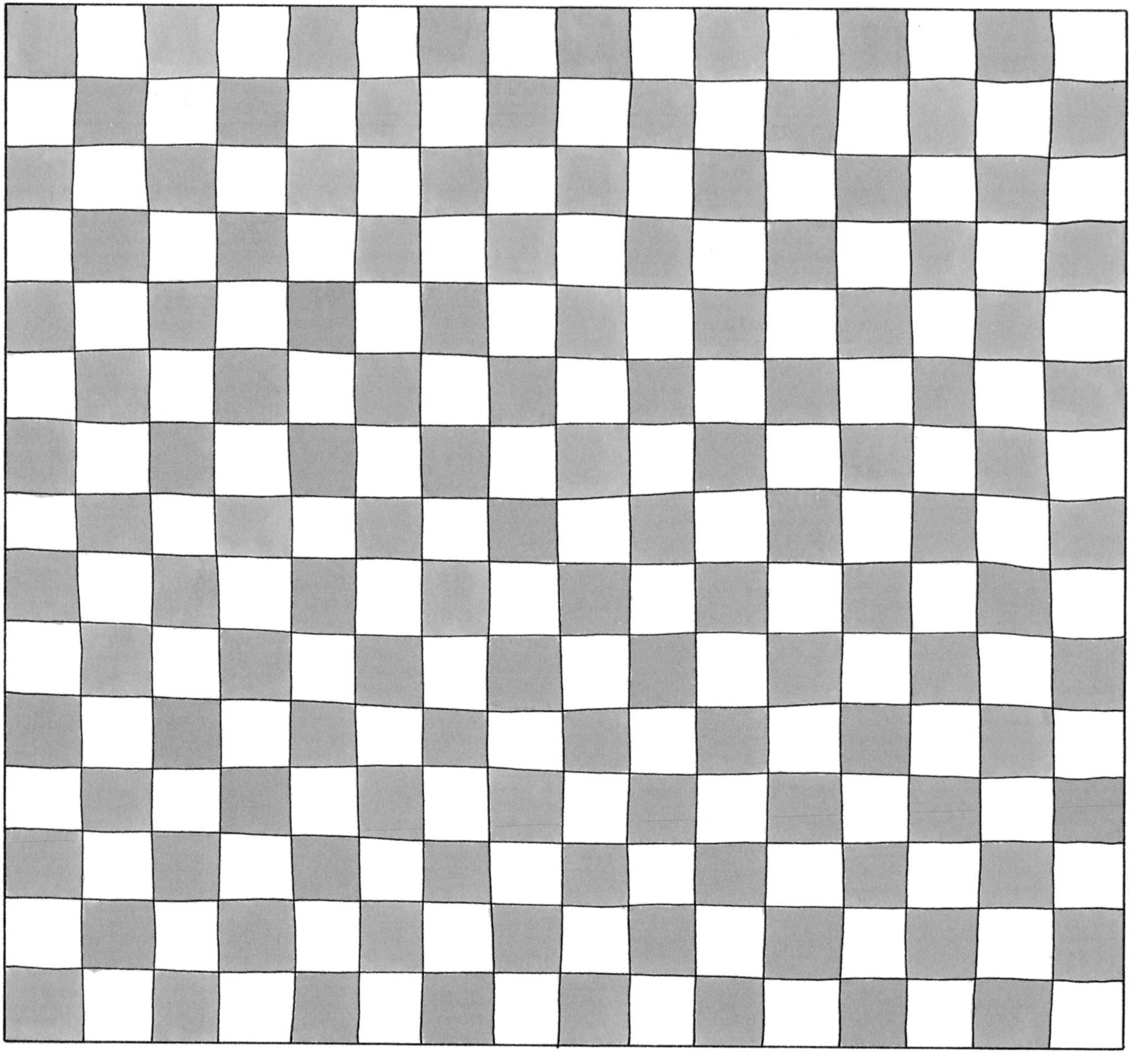

COOKIES AND CANDIES
BY BEN

I've been experimenting with cookies and candies in my ice cream since I was five years old. It seemed to me just the natural evolution of cookies and milk. The idea of eating two good things at one time was irresistible. It also gave me the opportunity to learn how to bite ice cream.

As I see it, there are three types of people who love ice cream: the lickers, the nibblers, and the biters. The lickers aren't very inhibited when it comes to wrapping their tongues around an ice cream cone. They're the sensual ones.

LICKER NIBBLER BITER

The nibblers are more proper—they wouldn't be caught doing anything in public that might embarrass themselves, their friends, or even complete strangers. They also always nibble with a napkin in hand.

The third group, of which I am a proud member, is made up of biters. We attack our ice cream with gusto, tend to eat it quickly, and inevitably, eat a lot more of it than the lickers or the nibblers.

Candy's Chocolate Candy

Ben's Chocolate Ice Cream
  (page 44)
¾ *cup coarsely chopped*
  bittersweet chocolate,
  such as Lindt

1 cup marshmallow topping

1. Prepare Ben's Chocolate Ice Cream.

2. After the ice cream stiffens (about 2 minutes before it is done), add the chocolate, then continue freezing until the ice cream is ready.

3. Remove the dasher and fold in the marshmallow topping with a spatula.

Makes generous 1 quart

Ben says:

Once, when I was a guest on a late-night radio talk show in Miami, a woman named Candy called in. She wanted to know how to make chocolate ice cream with chocolate chips and marshmallows. We discussed the merits of both mini marshmallows and marshmallow swirl but couldn't decide which would be best. We even took a poll among the listeners, but it was an even split. We finally decided on the marshmallow swirl for greater contrast.

Chocolate Reese's Cup

1 cup coarsely chopped Reese's Peanut Butter Cups

Ben's Chocolate Ice Cream (page 44)

1. Place the candy in a bowl, cover, and refrigerate.

2. Prepare Ben's Chocolate Ice Cream.

3. After the ice cream stiffens (about 2 minutes before it is done), add the candy, then continue freezing until the ice cream is ready.

Makes generous 1 quart

Reese's® Peanut Butter Cups® are manufactured by H.B. Reese Candy Company, a division of Hershey Foods Corporation.

After-Dinner Mint

French Vanilla or Light Chocolate Ice Cream (page 35 or 46)

¾ cup coarsely chopped Andes or other thin mints

1. Prepare the French Vanilla or Light Chocolate Ice Cream.

2. After the ice cream stiffens (about 2 minutes before it is done), add the mints, then continue freezing until the ice cream is ready.

Makes generous 1 quart

Kit Kat

Kit Kat® is manufactured by H.B. Reese Candy Company, a division of Hershey Foods Corporation.

The success of Kit Kat Ice Cream lies in the candy's construction. The chocolate seal around the wafers helps keep them crisp and crunchy in the ice cream.

4 Kit Kat candy bars   *2 teaspoons vanilla extract*
  (1.6 ounces each)
Sweet Cream Base (pages 28–29)

1. Using a sharp knife, cut the candy bars into bite-size pieces. Refrigerate in a covered bowl.

2. Prepare the Sweet Cream Base, adding the vanilla extract with the cream. Transfer to an ice cream maker and freeze following the manufacturer's instructions.

3. After the ice cream stiffens (about 2 minutes before it is done), add the chopped candy, then continue freezing until the ice cream is ready.

Makes generous 1 quart

Rolo Cup

Rolo® Cups are manufactured by Hershey Chocolate Company, a division of Hershey Foods Corporation.

Rolo Cups are good by themselves and great in ice cream. The liquid caramel center becomes delightfully crisp when blended into the freezing cream.

1 cup Rolo Cups   *Sweet Cream Base (pages 28–29)*
                                 2 teaspoons vanilla extract

1. About 1 hour before making the ice cream, place the Rolo cups in the freezer.

2. Prepare the Sweet Cream Base. Stir in the vanilla. Transfer the mixture to an ice cream maker and freeze following the manufacturer's directions.

3. When the ice cream begins to stiffen (about 5 minutes before it is done), cut the Rolo cups in half and add to the ice cream. Continue freezing until the ice cream is ready.

Makes generous 1 quart

Fifth Avenue

*1 cup coarsely chopped
  5th Avenue candy bars*

*Sweet Cream Base (pages 28–29)
2 teaspoons vanilla extract*

1. Place the candy in a bowl, cover, and refrigerate.

2. Prepare the Sweet Cream Base. Stir in the vanilla. Transfer to an ice cream maker and freeze following the manufacturer's instructions.

3. After the ice cream stiffens (about 2 minutes before it is done), add the candy, then continue freezing until the ice cream is ready.

Makes generous 1 quart

5th Avenue® is made by the confectionary division of Luden's, Inc.

Chocolate Gingersnap

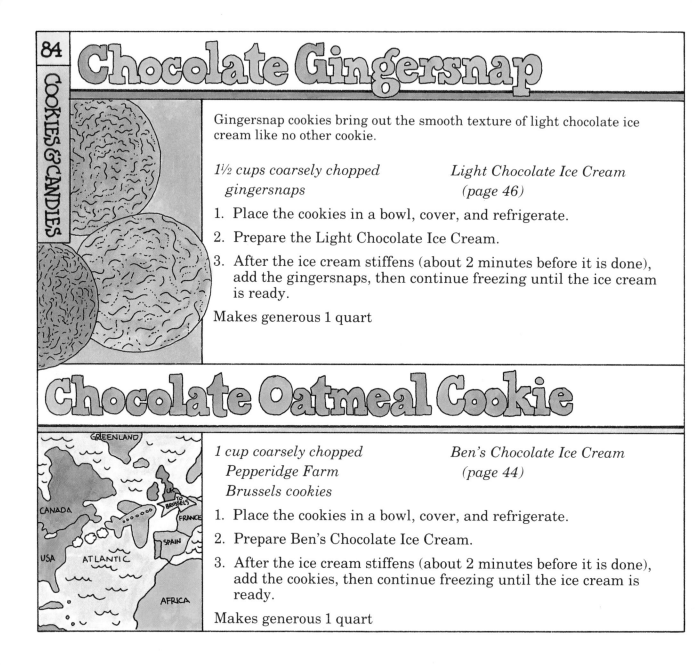

Gingersnap cookies bring out the smooth texture of light chocolate ice cream like no other cookie.

1½ cups coarsely chopped gingersnaps

Light Chocolate Ice Cream (page 46)

1. Place the cookies in a bowl, cover, and refrigerate.

2. Prepare the Light Chocolate Ice Cream.

3. After the ice cream stiffens (about 2 minutes before it is done), add the gingersnaps, then continue freezing until the ice cream is ready.

Makes generous 1 quart

Chocolate Oatmeal Cookie

1 cup coarsely chopped Pepperidge Farm Brussels cookies

Ben's Chocolate Ice Cream (page 44)

1. Place the cookies in a bowl, cover, and refrigerate.

2. Prepare Ben's Chocolate Ice Cream.

3. After the ice cream stiffens (about 2 minutes before it is done), add the cookies, then continue freezing until the ice cream is ready.

Makes generous 1 quart

Chocolate Mystic Mint

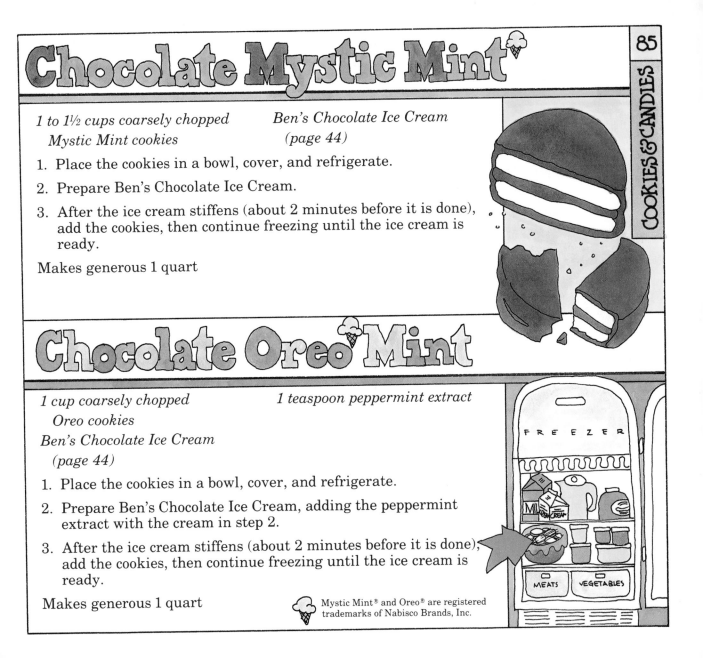

1 to 1½ cups coarsely chopped
  Mystic Mint cookies

Ben's Chocolate Ice Cream
  (page 44)

1. Place the cookies in a bowl, cover, and refrigerate.

2. Prepare Ben's Chocolate Ice Cream.

3. After the ice cream stiffens (about 2 minutes before it is done), add the cookies, then continue freezing until the ice cream is ready.

Makes generous 1 quart

Chocolate Oreo Mint

1 cup coarsely chopped
  Oreo cookies

Ben's Chocolate Ice Cream
  (page 44)

1 teaspoon peppermint extract

1. Place the cookies in a bowl, cover, and refrigerate.

2. Prepare Ben's Chocolate Ice Cream, adding the peppermint extract with the cream in step 2.

3. After the ice cream stiffens (about 2 minutes before it is done), add the cookies, then continue freezing until the ice cream is ready.

Makes generous 1 quart

Mystic Mint® and Oreo® are registered trademarks of Nabisco Brands, Inc.

Vanilla Superfudge Brownie

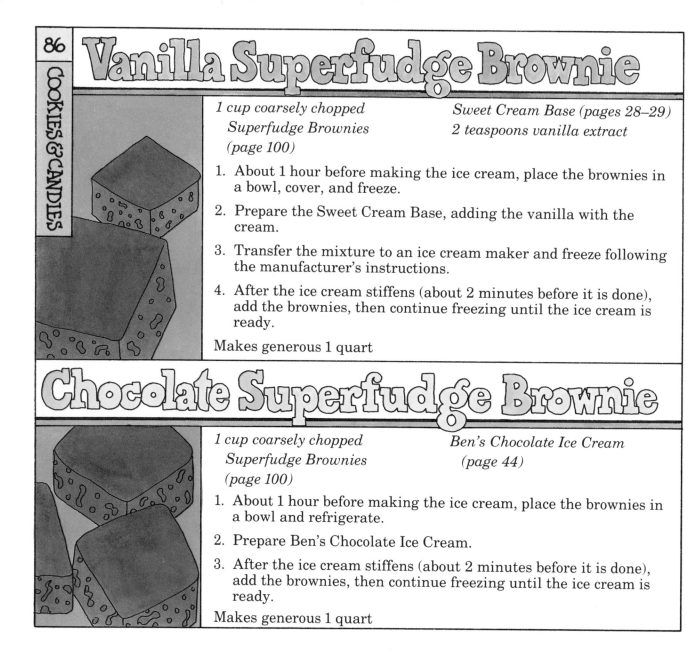

1 cup coarsely chopped
Superfudge Brownies
(page 100)

Sweet Cream Base (pages 28–29)
2 teaspoons vanilla extract

1. About 1 hour before making the ice cream, place the brownies in a bowl, cover, and freeze.

2. Prepare the Sweet Cream Base, adding the vanilla with the cream.

3. Transfer the mixture to an ice cream maker and freeze following the manufacturer's instructions.

4. After the ice cream stiffens (about 2 minutes before it is done), add the brownies, then continue freezing until the ice cream is ready.

Makes generous 1 quart

Chocolate Superfudge Brownie

1 cup coarsely chopped
Superfudge Brownies
(page 100)

Ben's Chocolate Ice Cream
(page 44)

1. About 1 hour before making the ice cream, place the brownies in a bowl and refrigerate.

2. Prepare Ben's Chocolate Ice Cream.

3. After the ice cream stiffens (about 2 minutes before it is done), add the brownies, then continue freezing until the ice cream is ready.

Makes generous 1 quart

Vanilla Fudge Chunk

We recommend Hilliard's Fudge, which we've found at country fairs around New England, but any favorite fudge will do.

*1 cup coarsely chopped good-
   quality fudge*

*Sweet Cream Base (pages 28–29)
2 teaspoons vanilla extract*

1. Place the fudge in a bowl, cover, and refrigerate.

2. Prepare the Sweet Cream Base. Stir in the vanilla. Transfer to an ice cream maker and freeze following the manufacturer's directions.

3. After the ice cream stiffens (about 2 minutes before it is done), add the fudge, then continue freezing until the ice cream is ready.

Makes generous 1 quart

VARIATION: Nutty Fudge Chunk

Add ¾ cup coarsely chopped nuts (any kind) with the fudge after the ice cream stiffens (about 2 minutes before it is done).

Vanilla M&M's

French Vanilla Ice Cream
(page 35)

¾ cup M & M's plain candies

1. Prepare the Sweet Cream Base. Transfer the mixture to an ice cream maker and freeze following the manufacturer's directions.

2. After the ice cream stiffens (about 2 minutes before it is ready), add the M & M's, then continue freezing until the ice cream is ready.

Makes generous 1 quart

M&M's® is distributed by M&M-Mars, a division of Mars, Inc.

Vanilla Oreo

1 cup coarsely chopped
Oreo cookies

Sweet Cream Base (pages 28–29)
2 teaspoons vanilla extract

1. Place the cookies in a bowl, cover, and refrigerate.

2. Prepare the Sweet Cream Base, adding the vanilla extract with the cream. Transfer to an ice cream maker and freeze following the manufacturer's instructions.

3. After the ice cream stiffens (about 2 minutes before it is done), add the cookies, then continue freezing until the ice cream is ready.

Makes generous 1 quart

Oreo® is a registered trademark of Nabisco Brands, Inc.

SORBETS

orbets are among the most delicious, most refreshing, and easiest desserts you can make in your ice cream maker. We make most of our sorbets during the summer months with fresh fruit, so for us, it's primarily a seasonal dessert. Nothing compares to a fresh raspberry sorbet in early August made with berries picked that same morning at Snow's farm in Stowe and served with a shot of Chianti drizzled on top.

If there is a special flavor or ingredient you would like to try—and we haven't included it here—go right ahead. It will probably work just fine and taste great. One of the good things about sorbets is their flexibility—you can make them with almost any ingredients you have on hand.

sor-bets

Sor-bayz

A Sorbet by Any Other Name...

Frankly, we always thought the French word "sorbet" was too foreign and classy for us, so for a long time we never called our sorbets "sorbets." First, we referred to them as Ices (until we discovered that ices come in such flavors as "Blue" or "Red"). Next, we tried naming them Fresh Fruit Ices and Frosted Fruit Specials, but that never really caught on. So many people were asking for sorbets, in the end, elegance prevailed.

Slushes are very refreshing summer shakes made with our sorbets and milk or water, depending on whether you like them creamy or icy. To make a slush, put all the ingredients in a blender and process on low speed for a few minutes. Any combination of flavors will work in a slush. Raspberry-strawberry is one of our favorites; we also like lemon-raspberry made with two parts raspberry sorbet to one part lemon sorbet.

Icy Slush

Process ¾ cup plus 2 tablespoons water and 1 cup plus 2 tablespoons sorbet in a blender.

Makes 2 cups

Creamy Slush

Process ½ cup milk, ½ cup water, and 1 cup of your favorite sorbet or combination of sorbets in a blender.

Makes 2 cups

Apricot Sorbet

1 pound fresh apricots, pitted
  and chopped
½ cup plus 2 tablespoons sugar
2 tablespoons corn syrup

3 tablespoons frozen orange juice
  concentrate
2½ cups cold water

1. Combine the apricots and sugar in a mixing bowl. Refrigerate covered at least 1 hour.

2. When ready to freeze the sorbet, mash the apricots until puréed. Add the corn syrup, juice concentrate, and water and stir until blended.

3. Transfer the mixture to an ice cream maker and freeze following the manufacturer's instructions.

Makes 1 quart

Fruit Juice Sorbets

To make sorbets from fruit juice—either fresh, frozen, or canned—simply pour the chilled juice into an ice cream maker and freeze following the manufacturer's instructions. Our favorite sorbets are cranberry and pineapple. Passion fruit juice also makes an amazing sorbet.

Kiwi Sorbet

We especially like the delightful green color of kiwi sorbet. It's a big summer seller in our scoop shops.

⅓ pound fresh kiwis, peeled and cut into small pieces
¾ cup sugar
Juice of 1 large or 2 medium lemons

½ cup melon liqueur, such as Midori
2 tablespoons light corn syrup
2 cups cold water

1. Combine the kiwis, sugar, and lemon juice in a mixing bowl. Refrigerate covered at least 1 hour.

2. When ready to freeze the sorbet, mash the kiwis until puréed. Add the liqueur, corn syrup, and water and stir until blended.

3. Transfer the mixture to an ice cream maker and freeze following the manufacturer's instructions.

Makes 1 quart

Raspberry Sorbet

The combination of red wine and raspberries is so stupendous that we always drizzle a little extra wine on top of each scoop. A generous shot of Chianti over raspberry sorbet creates a truly synergistic effect.

¾ pound fresh raspberries
1½ cups sugar
Juice of ½ lemon

¼ cup dry red wine
¼ cup light corn syrup
1 cup cold water

1. Combine the raspberries, sugar, and lemon juice in a mixing bowl. Refrigerate covered at least 1 hour.

2. When ready to freeze, add the red wine, corn syrup, and water and stir gently until blended.

3. Transfer the mixture to an ice cream maker and freeze following the manufacturer's instructions.

Makes 1 quart

Strawberry Sorbet

Strawberry sorbet is one of our best-selling summer flavors. Ben prefers this sweet version. Jerry likes to cut down on the sugar.

½ pound fresh strawberries,
hulled and sliced
¾ cup sugar

Juice of 1 large or 2
medium lemons
¼ cup corn syrup
2 cups cold water

1. Combine the strawberries, sugar, and lemon juice in a mixing bowl. Refrigerate covered at least 1 hour.

2. When ready to freeze the sorbet, mash the strawberries until puréed. Add the corn syrup and water and stir until blended.

3. Transfer the mixture to an ice cream maker and freeze following the manufacturer's instructions.

Makes 1 quart

Lemon Daiquiri

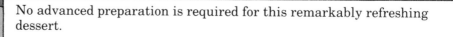

No advanced preparation is required for this remarkably refreshing dessert.

3 lemons, chilled
1 cup sugar
2 tablespoons rum

¼ cup corn syrup
2½ cups very cold water

1. Grate the zest from 1 lemon and set it aside.

2. Juice the lemons. Save the pulp but pick out the pits.

3. Stir the sugar, rum, corn syrup, and water together in a mixing bowl until the sugar dissolves. Stir in the lemon juice and zest.

4. Transfer the mixture to an ice cream maker and freeze following the manufacturer's instructions.

Makes 1 quart

Mimosa Ice

For Sunday brunch, we like to scoop mimosa ice into a glass of champagne or right into a mimosa cocktail (that makes a Mimosa Mimosa). We also add a generous number of scoops to the champagne punch on New Year's Eve.

1½ cups champagne
1½ cups orange juice

¼ cup sugar

1. Pour the champagne and orange juice into a large bowl. Add the sugar and stir until the sugar is dissolved and the champagne is flat.

2. Transfer the mixture to an ice cream maker and freeze following the manufacturer's instructions.

Makes 1 quart

Beer Sorbet

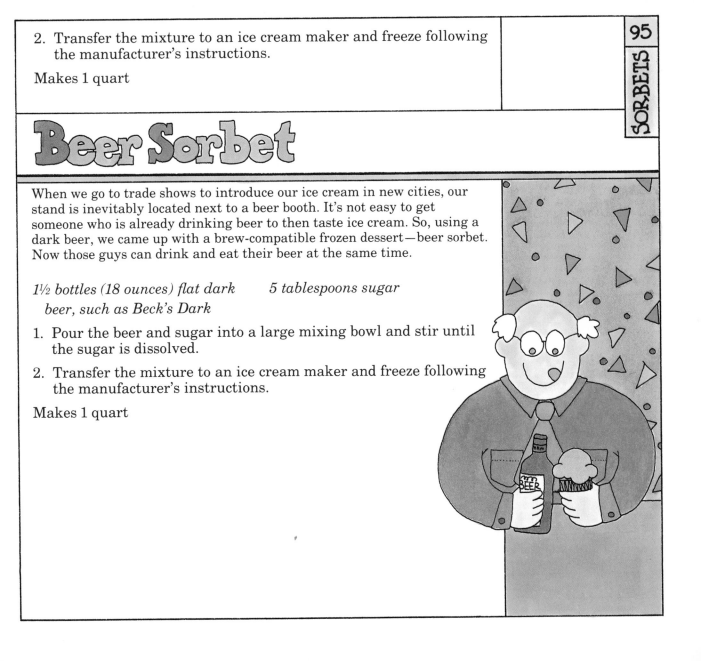

When we go to trade shows to introduce our ice cream in new cities, our stand is inevitably located next to a beer booth. It's not easy to get someone who is already drinking beer to then taste ice cream. So, using a dark beer, we came up with a brew-compatible frozen dessert—beer sorbet. Now those guys can drink and eat their beer at the same time.

1½ bottles (18 ounces) flat dark   *5 tablespoons sugar*
beer, such as Beck's Dark

1. Pour the beer and sugar into a large mixing bowl and stir until the sugar is dissolved.

2. Transfer the mixture to an ice cream maker and freeze following the manufacturer's instructions.

Makes 1 quart

THE BAKERY

hen it comes to custom-made desserts, we're very good at taking orders. In our bakery, we've created extravaganzas for every occasion — from the usual birthdays, weddings, and anniversaries, to less typical Winter and Summer Solstice events. Our ice cream cakes come in every shape imaginable — and the inscriptions, although sometimes of doubtful literary merit, are never censored.

Giant Chocolate Chip Cookies

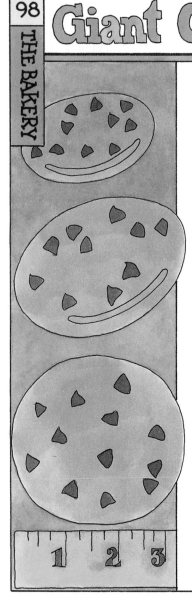

We like our chocolate chip cookies moist, chunky, and big—at least 3 inches across. A small ice cream scoop of dough will bake to about the right size. Of course, you don't have to bake the dough, you can use it instead to make a batch of Chocolate Chip Cookie Dough Ice Cream (page 63). If you have leftover cookies, chop them into small pieces and add to any flavor of homemade ice cream.

½ cup (1 stick) butter, at
   room temperature
¼ cup granulated sugar
⅓ cup brown sugar
1 large egg
½ teaspoon vanilla extract

1 cup plus 2 tablespoons
   all-purpose flour
½ teaspoon salt
½ teaspoon baking soda
1 cup semisweet chocolate chips
½ cup coarsely chopped walnuts

1. Preheat the oven to 350°F.

2. Beat the butter and both sugars in a large mixing bowl until light and fluffy. Add the egg and vanilla extract and mix well.

3. Mix the flour, salt, and baking soda in another bowl. Add the dry ingredients to the batter and mix until well blended. Stir in the chocolate chips and walnuts.

4. Drop the dough by small scoops 2 to 3 inches apart on an ungreased cookie sheet. Flatten each scoop with the back of a spoon to about 3 inches in diameter.

5. Bake until the centers are still slightly soft to the touch, 11 to 14 minutes. Let cool on the cookie sheet for 5 minutes, then transfer to racks to cool completely.

Makes 12 to 15 cookies

Giant Chocolate Chip Cookie Ice Cream Sandwich

It is possible to buy something like this in a store, but there is absolutely no comparison to the one you can make with fresh cookies and fresh ice cream. It's worth the effort.

1 scoop (about 4 ounces) French Vanilla Ice Cream (page 35), slightly softened

2 Giant Chocolate Chip Cookies (facing page)

Place the slightly softened ice cream on the bottom of one cookie and sandwich it with the second cookie.

Makes 1 serving

Superfudge Brownies

This recipe makes a light yet chewy fudge brownie. Almost a contradiction in terms, but it works if you do everything just right.

4 ounces unsweetened chocolate
½ cup (1 stick) butter
4 large eggs, at room
  temperature

½ teaspoon salt
2 cups sugar
1 teaspoon vanilla extract
1 cup all-purpose flour

1. Preheat the oven to 350°F. Butter and lightly flour a 13 x 9-inch baking pan.

2. Melt the chocolate and butter in the top of a double boiler over simmering water. Let cool in the pan to room temperature. If you're in a hurry, you can quickly cool it in the refrigerator, but be sure it doesn't get solid again.

3. Beat the eggs and salt in a mixing bowl until very fluffy. Gradually beat in the sugar and vanilla. Fold in the cooled chocolate mixture. Add the flour and fold just until blended. (It is important to fold in the chocolate and flour gently to keep the batter as fluffy as possible.)

4. Pour the batter into the prepared pan and smooth the top. Bake 25 to 30 minutes. Let cool in the pan completely before cutting.

Makes 9 brownies, 4 x 3 inches each

Blonde Brownies

½ cup (1 stick) butter, at room
  temperature
⅓ cup granulated sugar
½ cup brown sugar
1 large egg

½ teaspoon vanilla extract
1⅓ cups all-purpose flour
½ teaspoon salt
½ teaspoon baking soda

1. Preheat the oven to 350°F. Butter and lightly flour a
   13 x 9-inch baking pan.

2. Beat the butter and both sugars in a large mixing bowl until
   light and fluffy. Add the egg, vanilla, flour, salt, and baking
   soda and mix until well blended.

3. Spread the batter in the prepared pan. Bake 25 to 30 minutes.
   Let cool in the pan completely before cutting.

Makes 9 brownies, 4 x 3 inches each

VARIATION: Chocolate Chip Blonde Brownies

Stir 1½ cups semisweet chocolate chips into the batter.

Maple Walnut Brownies

Vermonters put maple syrup in everything from barbecue sauce to ice cream. We like it in our blonde brownies.

*1½ cups coarsely chopped
  walnuts*
*Blonde Brownies batter
  (page 101)*

*½ cup maple syrup, preferably
  Grade C*

1. Soak the walnuts in water to cover for 1 hour.

2. Preheat the oven to 350°F. Butter and lightly flour a 13 x 9-inch baking pan.

3. Prepare the brownies through step 2. Drain the walnuts. Add half the walnuts and all the maple syrup to the batter and stir until blended.

4. Spread the batter evenly in the prepared pans. Sprinkle the remaining walnuts over the batter and press in lightly.

5. Bake 25 to 30 minutes. Let cool in pan completely before cutting.

Makes 9 brownies, 4 x 3 inches each

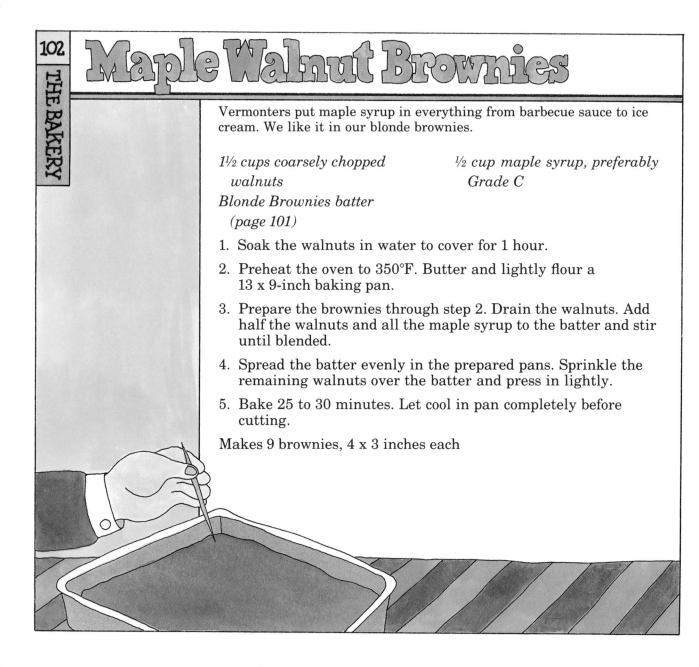

Chocolate Peanut-Butter Cup Brownies

For those of us who can't get enough peanut butter.

Superfudge Brownies batter
  (page 100)

32 to 35 miniature Reese's
  Peanut Butter Cups

1. Preheat the oven to 350°F. Butter and lightly flour a 13 x 9-inch baking pan.

2. Prepare the brownie batter. Spread the batter evenly in the prepared pans.

3. Cut 20 of the cups in half and arrange them evenly on top of the batter. Lightly press the cups into the batter.

4. Bake about 23 minutes. Place 1 whole peanut butter cup in the middle of each brownie-to-be. Return to the oven and bake 2 minutes. Let cool in the pan completely before cutting.

Makes 12 brownies, 3 x 3 inches each

Brownie Ice Cream Layer Cake

An incredibly delicious ice cream cake for births, birthdays, anniversaries, weddings, bar and bas mitzvahs, confirmations, and all other joyous events. All the ingredients should be well chilled before the final assembly. Whenever possible, freeze the cake pan for an hour or two before making the cake.

1 recipe Superfudge Brownies
(page 100)
1½ pints ice cream,
your favorite flavor

1 quart heavy or whipping
cream, cold
1 teaspoon vanilla extract
¼ cup confectioners' sugar

1. Prepare and bake the brownies in two 6-inch round pans. Let cool in pans completely.

2. Turn the brownie cakes out onto a cutting board. Spread a ¾-inch-thick layer of ice cream in a 6-inch round mold with 2-inch-high sides. Be sure not to leave any gaps. Layer 1 brownie cake on top of the ice cream and press it down firmly. Spread the remaining ice cream over the cake layer, leaving ½ inch at the top. Add the second cake layer, pressing it firmly on the ice cream.

3. Place the cake in the coldest spot in your freezer and freeze at least 2 hours.

4. When the cake is hard, remove it from the pan by placing the bottom of the pan in a basin of warm water for about a minute. Place the cake on a plate and freeze again until it is hard, about 10 minutes.

5. While you wait for the cake to harden, beat or whisk the cream, vanilla, and sugar in a large bowl until soft peaks form. (Be sure not to overbeat or you'll have butter.) Using a spatula, spread the whipped cream over the top and sides of the cake. Cut into wedges to serve. Congratulations!

Makes 8 servings

VARIATIONS GALORE:

For an even richer, more festive cake, top with Hot Fudge Sauce (page 120) and sprinkle with chopped walnuts. We have also used our Giant Chocolate Chip Cookies (page 98) in place of the brownies to make an ice cream cake. The choice is yours.

SUNDAES

& Concoctions

By Jerry

e usually take our ice cream straight because it just doesn't make sense to hide or disguise the taste of great ice cream. But should you wish to splurge, we've come up with these simple sundaes and concoctions. Needless to say, the Hot Fudge Sundae is a time-honored classic. Ben likes his with Mocha Walnut Ice Cream and whipped cream. I prefer Mint Oreo Ice Cream and whipped cream.

Fresh Whipped Cream

1 cup heavy or whipping cream, cold

2 tablespoons sugar (optional)

½ teaspoon vanilla extract (optional)

Beat the cream in a large chilled mixing bowl until it starts to thicken. Gradually add the sugar and vanilla, if using, while continuing to beat. The whipped cream is ready when it holds a stiff peak. Be sure not to overbeat or you'll have butter.

Makes 1 pint

Jerry says:

I like my whipped cream straight—just cream and nothing else—and easy. I pour the cold cream into a chilled bowl and whip it up with an electric beater. Ben, on the other hand, likes to add sugar and vanilla and beat it the old-fashioned way—with a whisk. He claims expending a little effort with this simple hand-held tool makes the cream taste better.

However you choose to make whipped cream, it helps to chill the mixing bowl and the whisk or beaters before beginning.

Fruit Lover's Frolic

3 scoops French Vanilla
  Ice Cream (page 35)
6 Bing cherries,
  halved and pitted

1 ripe medium peach, sliced
¼ cup fresh wild blueberries
Dollop Fresh Whipped Cream
  (facing page)

Scoop the ice cream into a dessert bowl. Top with the cherries, peach, and blueberries, then add a dollop of whipped cream.

Makes 1 serving

Chocolate Nut's Delight

This was one of the top two best-selling sundaes in our first store in the old gas station. At that time, we made it without green M & M's because they were Jerry's favorites and he always managed to get to them first.

3 scoops your favorite
  Chocolate Ice Cream
  (pages 44–46)
¼ cup good-quality
  chocolate syrup
¼ cup plus 2 tablespoons
  Hot Fudge Sauce (page 120)

2 to 4 tablespoons coarsely
  chopped walnuts
2 to 4 tablespoons coarsely
  chopped almonds
2 teaspoons plain chocolate
  M & M's

Scoop the ice cream into a dessert bowl. Top with the chocolate syrup, hot fudge, nuts, and M & M's.

Makes 1 serving

Chestnut Mare

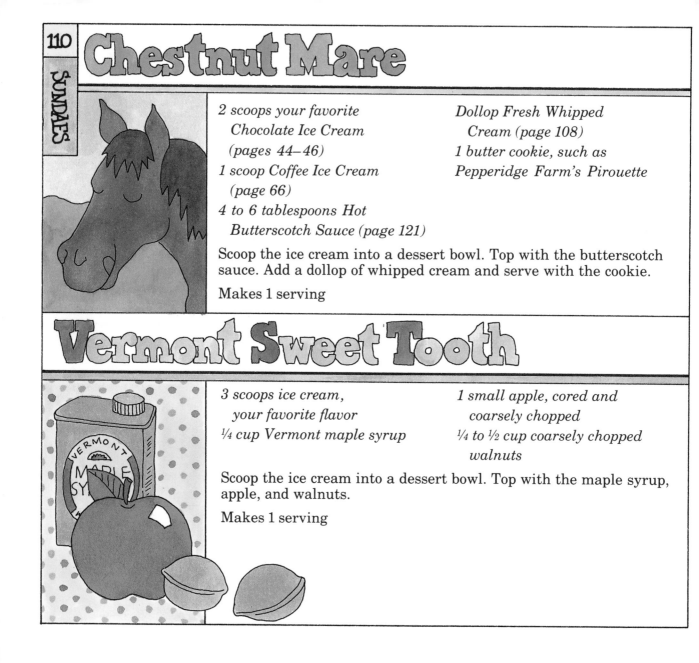

2 scoops your favorite
  Chocolate Ice Cream
  (pages 44–46)
1 scoop Coffee Ice Cream
  (page 66)
4 to 6 tablespoons Hot
  Butterscotch Sauce (page 121)

Dollop Fresh Whipped
  Cream (page 108)
1 butter cookie, such as
  Pepperidge Farm's Pirouette

Scoop the ice cream into a dessert bowl. Top with the butterscotch sauce. Add a dollop of whipped cream and serve with the cookie.

Makes 1 serving

Vermont Sweet Tooth

3 scoops ice cream,
  your favorite flavor
¼ cup Vermont maple syrup

1 small apple, cored and
  coarsely chopped
¼ to ½ cup coarsely chopped
  walnuts

Scoop the ice cream into a dessert bowl. Top with the maple syrup, apple, and walnuts.

Makes 1 serving

Minty Morsel

2 scoops your favorite Chocolate
  Ice Cream (pages 44-46)
1 scoop French Vanilla
  Ice Cream (page 35)
¼ to ½ cup crushed
  peppermint candies

¼ cup chocolate syrup
Dollop Fresh Whipped Cream
  (page 108)
1 butter cookie, such as
  Pepperidge Farm Pirouette

Scoop the ice cream into a dessert bowl. Sprinkle
with the crushed candies, add the chocolate syrup,
and top with a dollop of whipped cream.
Serve with the cookie.

Makes 1 serving

Healthfood Heaven

3 scoops ice cream,
  your favorite flavor
4 to 6 tablespoons granola

Dollop Fresh Whipped Cream
  (page 108)
1 strawberry for garnish
½ sliced banana

Scoop the ice cream into a dessert bowl. Sprinkle with the granola,
then add a dollop of whipped cream. Garnish with the strawberry
and banana.

Makes 1 serving

Charoses Special

A tribute to Rabbi Saperstein and our forefathers.

*3 scoops French Vanilla Ice
  Cream (page 35) or
  your favorite flavor*
2 tablespoons honey
2 tablespoons raisins

*2 tablespoons coarsely chopped
  walnuts*
*½ medium apple, cored
  and chopped*

Scoop the ice cream into a dessert bowl. Drizzle with the honey.
Sprinkle with the raisins and walnuts and finish off with a layer of
apple.

Makes 1 serving

Apple of Your Eye

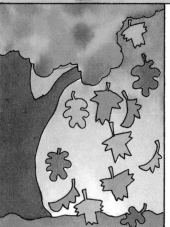

Another autumn specialty of our downtown store.

*3 scoops French Vanilla
  Ice Cream
  (page 35)*
*¼ cup Hot Honey Apple
  Cinnamon Raisin Topping
  (page 122)*

*Dollop Fresh Whipped Cream
  (page 108)*
½ to 1 banana, sliced

Scoop the ice cream into a dessert bowl. Add the hot honey topping.
Top with a dollop of whipped cream and garnish with enough
banana slices to make you happy.

Makes 1 serving

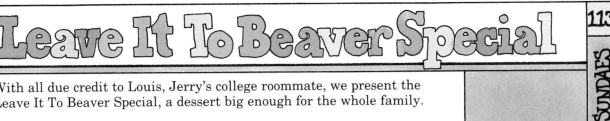

With all due credit to Louis, Jerry's college roommate, we present the Leave It To Beaver Special, a dessert big enough for the whole family.

4 scoops Fresh Peaches and Cream Ice Cream—The Cleavers (Fresh Georgia Peach Ice Cream, page 38, will do just fine.)

1 scoop French Vanilla Ice Cream (page 35)—Whitey

1 scoop Oreo Mint Ice Cream (page 41)—Eddie Haskell

¼ cup chopped mixed nuts, such as almonds and walnuts— Lumpy

¼ cup chocolate syrup

Dollop Fresh Whipped Cream (page 108)

Scoop the ice cream into a medium serving bowl. Top with the nuts, syrup, and whipped cream.

Makes enough to feed a Cleaver-size family

Hot Cherry Fudge Sundae

This is Jerry and Ben's all-time favorite sundae. Keep in mind that the cherry-to-fudge ratio can be adjusted to your taste.

2 scoops French Vanilla Ice Cream (page 35)
1 scoop Mocha Ice Cream (page 72)

¼ cup Hot Burgundy Cherries (recipe follows)
¼ cup Hot Fudge Sauce (page 120)
Dollop Fresh Whipped Cream (page 108)

Scoop the ice cream into a dessert bowl. Top with the burgundy cherries and fudge sauce and add a dollop of whipped cream.

Makes 1 serving

Hot Burgundy Cherries

This is the *only* sauce for perfect Cherries Jubilee. The key ingredient is the grated lemon zest.

1 can (16 ounces) dark sweet pitted cherries in juice or light syrup
1 tablespoon fresh lemon juice

2 teaspoons cornstarch
1 tablespoon water
Grated zest of 1 lemon

1. Drain the liquid from the cherries into a small saucepan. Add the lemon juice and heat over low heat until hot.

2. Stir the cornstarch and water together in a small bowl. Stir into the hot cherry juice and cook, stirring constantly, until thickened.

3. Add the cherries and lemon zest. Cook, stirring frequently, until cherries are heated through, 2 to 3 minutes. Serve hot.

Makes generous 1 pint

Flaming Cherries Jubilee

One New Year's Eve, we made Flaming Cherries Jubilee for 2,000 people in downtown Burlington. It was such a success that we repeated the event in Saratoga Springs and Minneapolis. It's easier than it sounds. Just put 75 gallons of ice cream in a tub, make 125 gallons of hot burgundy cherries, and ignite many bottles of brandy in a large vessel. This will create a nice blue aura. All in all, it's a spectacular sight.

*1 large scoop French Vanilla
   Ice Cream (page 35)*

*1 cup Hot Burgundy Cherries
   (facing page)*
¼ cup brandy

1. Scoop the ice cream into a sundae dish.

2. Heat the cherries in a small saucepan over low heat.

3. Warm the brandy in another small saucepan. Ignite the brandy and pour it over the cherries. When the flames die down, stir the sauce and pour it over the ice cream.

Makes 1 serving

The Jerry Berry

If you can fit all this into a parfait glass, you're a magician.

*2 tablespoons sliced fresh
  strawberries*
*1 small scoop French Vanilla
  Ice Cream (page 35)*
*¼ cantaloupe, peeled, seeded,
  and cubed*

2 tablespoons fresh blueberries
*1 small scoop Wild Blueberry Ice
  Cream (page 59)*
½ banana, sliced
*Dollop Fresh Whipped Cream
  (page 108)*
1 whole strawberry for garnish

1. Place the sliced strawberries in the bottom of a parfait glass. Add the vanilla ice cream and top with half the cantaloupe and all the blueberries.

2. Add the blueberry ice cream. Top with the banana and the remaining cantaloupe. Add a dollop of whipped cream and garnish with the whole strawberry.

Makes 1 serving

Vermonster

The key to the Vermonster is variety and volume. Work quickly so you don't end up with a bowl of melted ice cream.

20 scoops ice cream, any combination of flavors

4 bananas, sliced

1 Superfudge Brownie (page 100), broken into bite-size pieces

3 Giant Chocolate-Chip Cookies (page 98), broken into bite-size pieces

1 cup coarsely chopped walnuts

1 small chocolate bar (2 to 4 ounces), coarsely chopped

1 small pack (1.95 ounces) plain chocolate M & M's

1 small pack (1.6 ounces) Reese's Pieces

½ cup Hot Fudge Sauce (page 120)

Generous ½ cup whipped cream

8 fresh strawberries, cut in half

Alternate layers of ice cream and toppings, except the whipped cream and strawberries, in a chilled very large bowl. Finish off with a final layer of the toppings. Dollop with whipped cream and garnish with strawberries.

Makes 1 humongous serving or 4 to 6 reasonable servings

At our shop, we have a list posted of the people who have single-handedly conquered the Vermonster. If you are able to do so (and have witnesses who will confirm the feat), please send us written notification, properly witnessed and notarized. We will be happy to add your name to the list at our scoop shop in our Waterbury plant.

Fried Ice Cream

A good batch of fried ice cream is crunchy on the outside and cold and creamy on the inside. We developed this recipe after long hours of experimentation in the kitchen of some obliging friends. There are three key factors to making successful fried ice cream: Make sure the ice cream balls are frozen very hard, use cornflakes for insulation, and, most importantly, coat the ice cream balls completely with the batter to avoid any messy leaks.

1⅓ cups all-purpose flour
1 tablespoon sugar
1 teaspoon salt
1 tablespoon vegetable oil
2 egg yolks, lightly beaten
¾ cup flat beer

8 balls ice cream, any flavor
  (about 1 quart)
2 cups slightly crushed
  cornflakes
1 quart peanut oil
2 egg whites

1. The day before serving, make the batter: Mix the flour, sugar, salt, oil, and egg yolks in a mixing bowl. Gradually stir in the beer. Refrigerate covered overnight.

2. Also the day before serving, coat the ice cream balls thoroughly with crushed cornflakes. Place the ice cream balls in the coldest part of the freezer and freeze overnight.

3. When ready to serve, heat the peanut oil in a deep-fat fryer or in a deep pot to 375°F.

4. Beat the egg whites until stiff and fold into the batter.

5. Coat 2 or 3 of the ice cream balls completely and heavily with the batter and add to the hot oil. Turn up the heat to maintain a temperature of 375°F. Fry the ice cream until golden brown. Remove with a slotted spoon to paper towels. Drain briefly, then serve immediately. Repeat with the remaining ice cream balls.

Makes 4 servings

SAUCES

The art of preparing sauces and toppings is easy to learn and the rewards are great. The art of applying sauces and topping is the tricky part. Use restraint. Remember it is the homemade ice cream that is starring in this show.

Hot Fudge Sauce

When we first opened our shop, we couldn't find a decent commercial hot fudge sauce for our sundaes. Everything we tried was either overstabilized, made with corn syrup, or packed with preservatives. When we came up with this recipe, we found it was an immediate hit. We still make our own sauce because we haven't found one that is smoother, richer, or more velvety. It also lasts a long time, so store what's left in your refrigerator.

4 ounces unsweetened chocolate
½ cup (1 stick) butter
¾ cup unsweetened cocoa powder

2 cups sugar
½ cup milk
½ cup heavy or whipping cream

1. Melt the chocolate and butter, stirring frequently, in the top of a double boiler over simmering water. Add the cocoa and whisk until dissolved.

2. Using a slotted spoon, gradually stir in the sugar. (The mixture should be the consistency of wet sand.) Cook, stirring occasionally, over simmering water for 20 minutes. Check the water level in the double boiler occasionally and replenish if necessary.

3. Gradually stir in the milk and cream and keep stirring until completely blended. Continue cooking, stirring and checking the water occasionally, for 1 hour. The fudge is ready when it is completely smooth and all the sugar is dissolved.

Makes generous 1 quart

VARIATIONS: Peppermint Hot Fudge

It's easy to personalize a classic hot fudge sauce with these variations.

Add ¼ teaspoon peppermint extract.

Grand Marnier Hot Fudge

Add 3 tablespoons Grand Marnier.

Almond Hot Fudge

Add ½ teaspoon almond extract.

 Hot Butterscotch Sauce

Be prepared to serve all the butterscotch sauce you make because it doesn't keep very well. Ben suggests serving hot butterscotch sauce over generous scoops of coffee ice cream.

1 cup light corn syrup
1 cup brown sugar
4 tablespoons (½ stick)
  unsalted butter

Pinch salt
½ cup plus 2 tablespoons heavy
  or whipping cream

1. Place the corn syrup, sugar, butter, and salt in a medium saucepan. Heat, stirring occasionally, over low heat until blended and smooth. Increase the heat to medium and heat to boiling.

2. Remove from the heat and let stand 3 to 4 minutes to cool slightly. Gradually stir in the cream. Serve at once.

Makes about 1 pint

Hot Honey Apple Cinnamon Raisin Topping

The perfect fall topping for a scoop of homemade vanilla ice cream.

¼ cup (½ stick) butter
3 medium apples, peeled, cored and sliced (about 1½ cups)
⅓ cup apple cider

⅓ cup seedless raisins
1 tablespoon honey
½ teaspoon cinnamon
½ teaspoon pure vanilla extract

1. Melt the butter in a medium saucepan over medium-low heat. Add the apples and cider; cook, stirring occasionally, until the apples begin to soften, about 10 minutes.

2. Add the raisins, honey, cinnamon, and vanilla and stir until blended. Continue cooking about 5 minutes. Serve hot.

Makes 1½ pints

When we first opened our store in the old gas station, one of the nicest sights on cold winter days was our friend Debbie Comley at the stove, preparing a pot of Hot Honey Apple Cinnamon Raisin Topping. Debbie came up with this quintessential New England sauce just to have something to dribble over another of her favorite inventions—Maple Grape-Nut Ice Cream (page 71).

Jerry's Jumbo Shake

When ice cream gets too icy, shakes are the answer. We don't use any syrups when we make them in our stores because our ice cream is so strongly flavored. But if you prefer, you can add some chocolate sauce, Kahlúa, coffee extract, or instant coffee.

1 cup (2 scoops) ice cream,   *¾ to 1 cup milk*
  your favorite flavor

Scoop the ice cream into a chilled metal shaker or blender. Add the milk. Mix or blend on low speed until thick and smooth.

Makes 1 serving

Ice Cream Soda

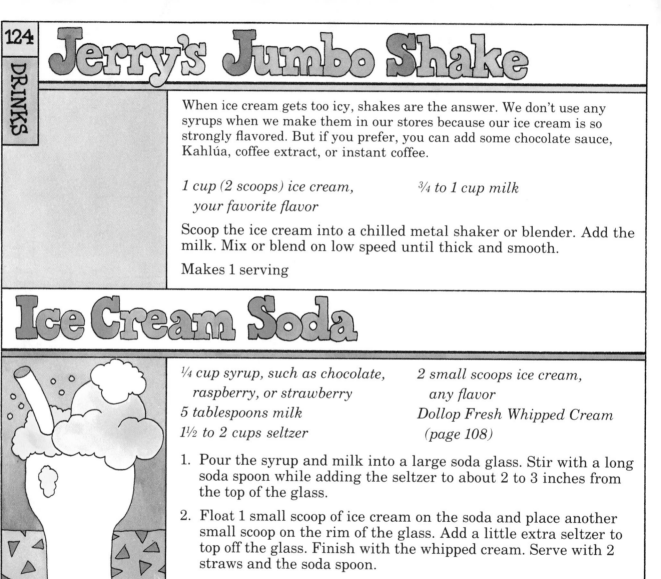

¼ cup syrup, such as chocolate,   *2 small scoops ice cream,*
  raspberry, or strawberry   *any flavor*
5 tablespoons milk   *Dollop Fresh Whipped Cream*
1½ to 2 cups seltzer   *(page 108)*

1. Pour the syrup and milk into a large soda glass. Stir with a long soda spoon while adding the seltzer to about 2 to 3 inches from the top of the glass.

2. Float 1 small scoop of ice cream on the soda and place another small scoop on the rim of the glass. Add a little extra seltzer to top off the glass. Finish with the whipped cream. Serve with 2 straws and the soda spoon.

Makes 1 serving

Hot Chocolate Float

Our hot chocolate is a true hot chocolate, not a hot cocoa. The extra cocoa fat in the hot fudge sauce makes for a richer smoother drink. We like to top it off with ice cream, fresh whipped cream, and shaved chocolate.

*2 tablespoons Hot Fudge Sauce
   (page 120)*
¾ cup milk
*1 small scoop ice cream,
   your favorite flavor*
*Dollop Fresh Whipped Cream
   (page 108)*

*1 ounce semisweet or
   bittersweet chocolate, shaved
   (we use Hershey's Special
   Dark Chocolate)*

1. Measure the fudge sauce into a large coffee cup or mug.

2. Heat the milk in a small saucepan over low heat. Do not boil. Pour the hot milk into the cup and stir until completely blended. Gingerly scoop the ice cream on top. Top with the whipped cream and sprinkle with the shaved chocolate.

Makes 1 serving

INDEX

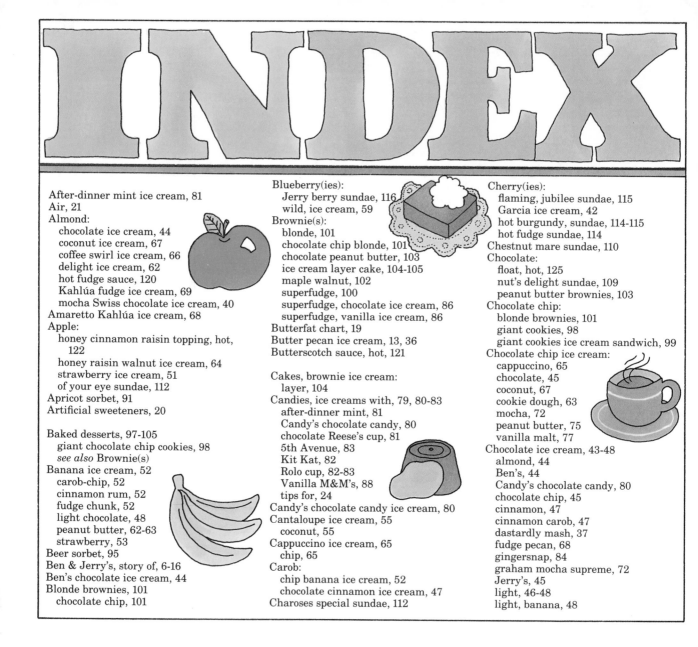

After-dinner mint ice cream, 81
Air, 21
Almond:
    chocolate ice cream, 44
    coconut ice cream, 67
    coffee swirl ice cream, 66
    delight ice cream, 62
    hot fudge sauce, 120
    Kahlúa fudge ice cream, 69
    mocha Swiss chocolate ice cream, 40
Amaretto Kahlúa ice cream, 68
Apple:
    honey cinnamon raisin topping, hot, 122
    honey raisin walnut ice cream, 64
    strawberry ice cream, 51
    of your eye sundae, 112
Apricot sorbet, 91
Artificial sweeteners, 20

Baked desserts, 97-105
    giant chocolate chip cookies, 98
    see also Brownie(s)
Banana ice cream, 52
    carob-chip, 52
    cinnamon rum, 52
    fudge chunk, 52
    light chocolate, 48
    peanut butter, 62-63
    strawberry, 53
Beer sorbet, 95
Ben & Jerry's, story of, 6-16
Ben's chocolate ice cream, 44
Blonde brownies, 101
    chocolate chip, 101

Blueberry(ies):
    Jerry berry sundae, 116
    wild, ice cream, 59
Brownie(s):
    blonde, 101
    chocolate chip blonde, 101
    chocolate peanut butter, 103
    ice cream layer cake, 104-105
    maple walnut, 102
    superfudge, 100
    superfudge, chocolate ice cream, 86
    superfudge, vanilla ice cream, 86
Butterfat chart, 19
Butter pecan ice cream, 13, 36
Butterscotch sauce, hot, 121

Cakes, brownie ice cream:
    layer, 104
Candies, ice creams with, 79, 80-83
    after-dinner mint, 81
    Candy's chocolate candy, 80
    chocolate Reese's cup, 81
    5th Avenue, 83
    Kit Kat, 82
    Rolo cup, 82-83
    Vanilla M&M's, 88
    tips for, 24
Candy's chocolate candy ice cream, 80
Cantaloupe ice cream, 55
    coconut, 55
Cappuccino ice cream, 65
    chip, 65
Carob:
    chip banana ice cream, 52
    chocolate cinnamon ice cream, 47
Charoses special sundae, 112

Cherry(ies):
    flaming, jubilee sundae, 115
    Garcia ice cream, 42
    hot burgundy, sundae, 114-115
    hot fudge sundae, 114
Chestnut mare sundae, 110
Chocolate:
    float, hot, 125
    nut's delight sundae, 109
    peanut butter brownies, 103
Chocolate chip:
    blonde brownies, 101
    giant cookies, 98
    giant cookies ice cream sandwich, 99
Chocolate chip ice cream:
    cappuccino, 65
    chocolate, 45
    coconut, 67
    cookie dough, 63
    mocha, 72
    peanut butter, 75
    vanilla malt, 77
Chocolate ice cream, 43-48
    almond, 44
    Ben's, 44
    Candy's chocolate candy, 80
    chocolate chip, 45
    cinnamon, 47
    cinnamon carob, 47
    dastardly mash, 37
    fudge pecan, 68
    gingersnap, 84
    graham mocha supreme, 72
    Jerry's, 45
    light, 46-48
    light, banana, 48

light, nutty fudge chunk, 48
malt, 47
mandarin, 48
mint, 47
Mystic Mint, 85
New York super fudge chunk, 34-35
oatmeal cookie, 84
Oreo mint, 85
peanut butter, 47
Reese's cup, 81
superfudge brownie, 86
Swiss, mocha almond, 40
Chunk(s), 11
  see also Fudge Chunk
Cinnamon:
  carob chocolate ice cream, 47
  chocolate ice cream, 47
  honey apple raisin topping, hot, 122
  rum banana ice cream, 52
Coconut ice cream, 67
  almond, 67
  cantaloupe, 55
  chip, 67
  rum, 67
  strawberry, 58-59
Coffee ice cream, 66
  almond swirl, 66
  cappuccino, 65
  Heath Bar crunch, 33
  see also Mocha ice cream
Coheeni's First Law of Ice-Cream Eating
  Dynamics, 7-8
Cold Hollow Cider Mill, 64, 71
Cookies, giant chocolate chip, 98
  ice cream sandwich, 99
Cookies, ice cream with, 79, 84-85
  chocolate gingersnap, 84
  chocolate Mystic Mint, 85
  chocolate oatmeal, 84
  chocolate Oreo mint, 85
  tips for, 24
  vanilla Oreo, 88
Corn syrup, 20
Creamy slush, 90

Daiquiri lemon sorbet, 94
Dastardly mash ice cream, 37
Drink(s), 123-125
  creamy slush, 90

hot chocolate float, 125
ice cream soda, 124
icy slush, 90
Jerry's jumbo shake, 124

Egg nog ice cream, 76
Eggs, 20-21

5th Avenue ice cream, 83
Flaming cherries jubilee sundae, 115
Flavorings, 22
Float, hot chocolate, 125
French vanilla ice cream, 35
Fried ice cream, 118
Fruit ice creams, 49-59
  apple honey raisin walnut, 64
  apple strawberry, 51
  banana, 52
  banana strawberry, 53
  cantaloupe, 55
  fresh Georgia peach, 38
  kiwi, 56-57
  orange cream dream, 56
  plum, 57
  pumpkin, 58
  raspberry, 39
  strawberry, 54
  strawberry coconut, 58-59
  sweetening fruit in, 50
  tips for, 23
  wild blueberry, 59
Fruit juice sorbets, 90
Fruit lover's frolic sundae, 109
Fudge:
  cherry sundae, hot, 114
  chocolate, pecan ice cream, 68
  Kahlúa almond ice cream, 69
  superfudge brownies, 100
  swirl peanut butter ice cream, 75
  see also Hot fudge sauces
Fudge chunk:
  banana ice cream, 52
  light chocolate nutty ice cream, 48
  mocha ice cream, 73
  New York super, ice cream, 34-35
  nutty ice cream, 87
  vanilla ice cream, 87

Giant chocolate chip cookies, 98

ice cream sandwich, 99
Gingersnap chocolate ice cream, 84
Graham chocolate mocha supreme ice
  cream, 72
Grand Marnier hot fudge sauce, 120
Grape-Nuts maple ice cream, 71

Hard vs. soft ice cream, 22
Healthfood heaven sundae, 111
Heath Bar(s), 24
  coffee crunch ice cream, 33
  crunch ice cream, 32
  mocha crunch ice cream, 73
Honey:
  apple cinnamon raisin
    topping, hot, 122
  apple raisin walnut ice cream, 64
  as sweetener, 20, 65
Hot:
  burgundy cherries, 114-15
  butterscotch sauce, 121
  cherry fudge sundae, 114
  chocolate float, 125
  honey apple cinnamon raisin
    topping, 122
Hot fudge sauces, 120
  almond, 120
  Grand Marnier, 120
  peppermint, 120

Ice cream making, 18-24
  air as hidden ingredient in, 21
  with cookies and candies, 24
  eggs in, 20-21
  flavorings in, 22
  with fruit, 23
  ice crystals in, 21-22
  liqueurs in, 23
  pint-size batches in, 25
  problems in, 21
  salt in, 22
  sweet cream bases for, 18-19, 28-29
  sweeteners in, 20, 50, 65
  see also specific flavors
Ice cream sandwich, giant
  chocolate chip cookies, 99
Ice crystals, 21-22
Icy slush, 90
Ingredients, 18-24

Jerry berry sundae, 116
Jerry's chocolate ice cream, 45

Kahlúa ice cream:
    almond fudge, 69
    amaretto, 68
    Kit Kat ice cream, 82
Kiwi:
    ice cream, 56-57
    sorbet, 92
Leave It To Beaver special, 113
Lemon daiquiri sorbet, 94
Light chocolate ice cream, 46-48
    banana, 48
    nutty fudge chunk, 48
Liqueur, 23

Malt:
    chocolate, ice cream, 47
    vanilla, chip ice cream, 77
Mandarin chocolate ice cream, 48
M&M's vanilla ice cream, 88
Maple:
    Grape-Nuts ice cream, 71
    syrup, as sweetener, 20
    syrup chart, 71
    walnut brownies, 102
    walnut ice cream, 70
Mimosa ice, 94-95
Mint:
    after-dinner, ice cream, 81
    chocolate ice cream, 47
    chocolate Mystic Mint ice cream, 85
    chocolate Oreo ice cream, 85
    Oreo ice cream, 41
Minty morsel sundae, 111
Mocha ice cream, 72-73
    chip, 72
    chocolate graham supreme, 72
    fudge chunk, 73
    Heath Bar crunch, 73
    Swiss chocolate almond, 40
    walnut, 73
Mystic Mint chocolate ice cream, 85

New York super fudge chunk
    ice cream, 34-35

Nutty fudge chunk ice cream, 87

Oatmeal cookie chocolate ice cream, 84
Orange cream dream ice cream, 56
Oreo:
    chocolate mint ice cream, 85
    mint ice cream, 41
    vanilla ice cream, 88

Peach ice cream, fresh Georgia, 38
Peanut brittle ice cream, 74
Peanut butter chocolate brownies, 103
Peanut butter ice cream, 74-75
    banana, 62-63
    chocolate, 47
    chocolate chip, 75
    chocolate Reese's cup, 81
    fudge swirl, 75
Pecan:
    butter, ice cream, 36
    chocolate fudge ice cream, 68
Peppermint hot fudge sauce, 120
Pint-size batches, 25
Plum ice cream, 57
Pumpkin ice cream, 58

Raisin:
    honey apple cinnamon topping, hot, 122
    honey apple walnut ice cream, 64
Raspberry:
    ice cream, 39
    sorbet, 92-93
Rolo cup ice cream, 82-83
Rum coconut ice cream, 67

Salt, 22
Sauces, 119-122
    hot butterscotch, 121
    hot honey apple cinnamon raisin
        topping, 122
    see also Hot fudge sauces
Scooping, 10
Shakes:
    Jerry's jumbo, 124
    sorbet slushes, 90
Soda, ice cream, 124
Soft vs. hard ice cream, 22
Sorbet(s), 89-95
    apricot, 91

beer, 95
fruit juice, 90
kiwi, 82
lemon daiquiri, 94
mimosa ice, 94-95
raspberry, 92-93
slushes, 90
strawberry, 93
Strawberry ice cream, 54
    apple, 51
    banana, 53
    coconut, 58-59
Strawberry sorbet, 93
Sundae(s), 107-118
    apple of your eye, 113
    charoses special, 112
    chestnut mare, 110
    chocolate nut's delight, 109
    flaming cherries jubilee, 115
    fruit lover's frolic, 109
    healthfood heaven, 111
    hot burgundy cherries, 114-115
    hot cherry fudge, 114
    Jerry berry, 116
    Leave It to Beaver special, 113
    minty morsel, 111
    Vermonster, 117
    Vermont sweet tooth, 110
    world's largest, 12
Superfudge brownie(s), 100
    chocolate ice cream, 86
    vanilla ice cream, 86
Sweet cream bases, 18-19, 28-29
Sweeteners, 20, 65
    for fruit-flavored ice creams, 50

Vanilla ice cream:
    French, 35
    fudge chunk, 87
    malt chip, 77
    M&M's, 88
    Oreo, 88
    superfudge brownie, 86
Vermonster, 117
Vermont sweet tooth sundae, 110